DISCARDED

COLLECTING
PRINTS

D1525611

Leila Lyons

HOUSE OF COLLECTIBLES
NEW YORK TORONTO LONDON SYDNEY AUCKLAND

REF
769.12
LYO

Copyright © 2006 by Leila Lyons

Important Notice: All the information, including valuations, in this book has been compiled from reliable sources, and efforts have been made to eliminate errors and questionable data. Nevertheless, the possibility of error, in a work of such immense scope, always exists. The publisher will not be responsible for any losses that may occur in the purchase, sale, or other transaction of items because of information contained herein. Readers who feel they have discovered errors are invited to write and inform us, so they may be corrected in subsequent editions.

All rights reserved. No part of this book may be reproduced in any form or by any means, electronic or mechanical, including photocopying, recording, or by any information storage and retrieval system, without the written permission of the publisher. Published in the United States by House of Collectibles, an imprint of The Random House Information Group, a division of Random House, Inc., New York, and simultaneously in Canada by Random House of Canada Limited, Toronto.

House of Collectibles and colophon are registered trademarks of Random House, Inc.

RANDOM HOUSE is a registered trademark of Random House, Inc.

This book is available at special discounts for bulk purchases for sales promotions or premiums. Special editions, including personalized covers, excerpts of existing books, and corporate imprints, can be created in large quantities for special needs. For more information, write to Special Markets/Premium Sales, 1745 Broadway, MD 6-2, New York, NY, 10019 or e-mail *specialmarkets@randomhouse.com*.

Please address inquiries about electronic licensing of any products for use on a network, in software, or on CD-ROM to the Subsidiary Rights Department, Random House Information Group, fax 212-572-6003.

Visit the House of Collectibles Web site: www.houseofcollectibles.com

Library of Congress Cataloging-in-Publication Data

Lyons, Leila.
    Instant expert : collecting prints / Leila Lyons.
        p. cm.
    Includes bibliographical references and index.
    ISBN 0-375-72056-1
      1. Prints—Collectors and collecting. 2. Prints—Expertising.
3. Prints—Technique. I. Title.

NE885.L96 2006
769'.12—dc22   2005052730

ISBN-10: 0-375-72056-1
ISBN-13: 978-0-375-72056-7

Printed in the United States of America

10 9 8 7 6 5 4 3 2 1

CONTENTS

For Charles, Chris, and Jamie always.

ACKNOWLEDGMENTS

The author would like to thank Chinley Chang, David Fandetta, Thomas French, Michael Graves, Michael Grover, J. P. Hayden, Lauren Kramer, Jennifer Landers, Jamie and Dana Lyons, Amanda Rinder, Rick Scott, Sarah Stratton, and, of course, the staff at Random House.

INTRODUCTION

If you enjoy people—their history, their personalities, their concerns, and their aspirations—you will love prints. From the invention of the printing press through the advent of modern digital imagery, graphics (the art world's term for original prints) have been the medium of the rich and the poor, of the powerful as well as the man in the street. Prints document persons of import, places of note, voyages of discovery, wondrously strange plants, birds and animals, flights of fashion or fancy, abstract and imaginative explorations, and architectural innovations. They provide an eye on the world, reflected through the prevailing styles of the day: Classical, Renaissance, Baroque, Realism, Abstract, Art Nouveau, Art Deco, Modernism. At a time when few could read, a picture was truly worth a thousand words and subsequent generations continued to enjoy these visual images, even after the invention of the camera and the introduction of television and the personal computer.

One of the joys of collecting art is that it is never static. Just when you are comfortable, you discover that art is forever changing. New faces, new ideas and new techniques can appear overnight. The standards that differentiate good art from bad art change over time. Public tastes change and personal preferences evolve, and the marketplace reflects the appreciation and/or depreciation these changes bring.

Art is very personal. Any piece of art will affect you in one way or another, either positively or negatively. As we look, we learn to differentiate between what speaks to us and what doesn't. Even the art we don't like can teach us a great deal. It doesn't matter where you start—just jump in!

Prints and print collectors tend to fall into two major categories. Decorative prints are those that, because of their great beauty and design, give visual pleasure and convey their message without particular regard to the artist's importance. Fine art or master prints, while also quite beautiful, are valued for the uniqueness and originality of the composition, the importance of the artist, the limited size of the edition and the skill exhibited in executing that particular image.

Just as there are many styles of graphics, there are many ways of collecting them. Print collectors and dealers tend to specialize in either antique prints or modern graphics. This is not wholly a matter of arbitrary choice, since the reference books and auction records upon which the expert relies have very specific beginning and ending dates. However, the two categories are in no way mutually exclusive. Many of us with eclectic tastes collect in both areas. The important thing is to collect what speaks to you personally and is in the best condition you can find in the marketplace at the time.

This book is not meant to be a definitive study. It is not a history of artistic styles, a complete dictionary of terms and processes, or an exhaustive price guide. Much has been left out for purposes of balancing wide coverage and conciseness. It is, however, an introduction to the kind of things that opened the door to the great enjoyment my family and I have experienced in the process of building our own collection. In this book you will find a brief history of graphics and the processes and terms used in printing, as well as some helpful directions on collecting and on caring for and evaluating your purchases. As you begin to develop your own collection you will no doubt have much to add.

What is an "instant expert"? An instant expert is one who is willing to develop an "educated eye." The educated eye is not a product of professional training as much as it is of experience, knowledge and an open mind. The instant expert is constantly looking at art, comparing and contrasting composition and technique, asking questions, and evaluating responses. He is not afraid to learn from his mistakes and enjoy his successes, and understands that collecting is not only a financial but an aesthetic investment, with the emotional rewards often outweighing the monetary appreciation.

No single volume can make you an expert instantly, but my hope is that this one will give you a starting point to begin your explorations. Expertise is a combination of knowledge and experience. Look at as many graphics as you can, ask as many questions as you can, and don't be afraid to test your own judgment.

1

A PRINTS PRIMER: TERMS AND TECHNIQUES

In earlier times a primer was the primary text that provided an introduction to the basics of a subject. This chapter introduces the processes and techniques used in graphic art. We'll look at the basic processes such as relief, intaglio, and stencil, and then their particular kinds, such as engraving, silk screening, and so on. A knowledge of these terms will help you choose the kinds of prints you find most attractive. You'll also be more comfortable visiting a gallery when you sound like you know what you're doing!

THE FIVE P's

Our Prints Primer begins with five P's: **people**, **paper**, **presses**, **processes**, and **periods**. All are integral to our understanding of this subject and all are insepa-

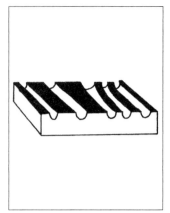 

Left:
Relief

Right:
Intaglio

rably linked throughout the five hundred and fifty years that the graphic arts have flourished.

Prints have always been the medium of the **people**. They provided visual representations that told a story without the need of words. Whether they made the Bible more meaningful, showed you a world beyond your imagination, demonstrated a new use for an old favorite plant, or depicted a fantastically plumed newly discovered bird, they caught the interest of the rich and poor alike. Centuries later, prints still have the ability to convey a message or lead us to explore an idea through either conventional or unconventional imagery.

Today we buy and dispose of copious amounts of **paper** casually and indiscriminately, but paper has not always been so plentiful. The making of paper was once a carefully guarded secret and, until fairly recently, it was a frightfully laborious and expensive product to produce. Without this monumental discovery, the world as we know it today might look entirely different.

We are so accustomed to the speed and clarity of today's digital printing that it is hard to comprehend the time and physical strength it took to transfer an image to paper in the early years of the printing **press**. The fact that the prints that have survived are still so highly valued is a testament to the skill and

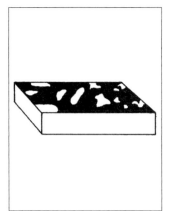 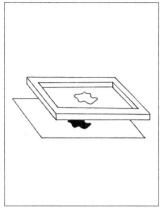

dedication of Johannes Gutenberg (c. 1398–1468), William Caxton (1422–1491), and other early printers. The development of the printing press in the fifteenth century was surely one of the most significant contributions to the modern world.

Left: Planographic

Right: Stencil

There are many specific terms for the various graphic **processes**, but there are basically only a few actual printing techniques: A **relief** process cuts away from the design, leaving a raised outline. An **intaglio** process cuts the design into the surface of the plate, leaving the outline submerged. A **planographic** process neither raises nor lowers the design into the surface of the plate, but draws on the plate with a substance that will hold ink. A **stencil** draws the design onto the medium, blocking part of the surface and leaving the open areas to be inked. Photomechanical processes transfer a design by means of a lens. In each of these printing processes, the medium onto which the design is placed is called the **matrix**. The matrix can be a metal plate, a block of wood, a stone—virtually anything that will not fall apart in the printing process. Specific types of these processes will be introduced and explained below.

Just as styles in fashion change from year to year, so too do the styles and subjects depicted in art. We speak of these trends in art history as **periods** and assign them a time span in which they flourished—for example, the Baroque, which lasted from about 1590 to about 1725—but these dates are not absolute. Many styles and periods overlap or run side by side—and there will be more yet to come. (Please see chapter two, "A Brief History of Graphic Arts.")

The development and availability of paper, coupled with the technical advancements in printing presses, created sophisticated techniques and skillfully rendered images that allowed every man to be an integral part of the constantly expanding and changing universe that surrounded him. The art that occurred from this combination, called a print or graphic, added a whole new dimension to the lives of everyday people and the world of fine art.

WHAT ARE THE PROCESSES USED IN PRINTING?

As mentioned earlier, all original prints are variations of five basic methods of printing. In relief printing, the artist's design is meant to stand clearly away from the background, providing a striking contrast of light and shadow. The lines are drawn onto the matrix and each side of the outline is carved away, leaving the image raised. The plate is then inked, and when paper is pressed to the block, the image is transferred to the paper.

In the intaglio process, the lines of the artist's design are cut or bitten into the matrix so that they lie beneath the surface. When the plate is inked and wiped clean, the ink remains in the cuts. When dampened paper is applied under pressure to the plate, it will draw the ink from the cuts and transfer the design to the paper.

In the planographic process, the artist's design is drawn on to the matrix with a waxy crayon-like substance, and the remaining surface is bathed in acid. This leaves the design slightly elevated by the wax but pits the rest of the matrix so that it can retain water when dampened. When an oily ink is applied, it sticks to the crayon outline but not to the wet background. Paper is then laid over the image, pressure applied from a roller, and the image is transferred.

Stencils are a device used for creating a design that duplicates color uniformly. The artist's design is separated into areas where specific colors are to appear, and these areas are transferred to a thin matrix. The areas to be inked are cut out (separate stencils for each color or gradation), and the remaining areas are left blocked out. Color is brushed across the stencil and transferred onto the paper beneath.

Following the introduction of the camera in the nineteenth century and the rapid advancement of technology in the twentieth, there have appeared in the marketplace several variations of the photomechanical process. In this reproductive process, an image is transferred from a design on a disk, paper, film, or other substance to a positive or negative film. A measured amount of light through the negative exposes the design onto a photo-sensitive plate. The exposure to light creates a chemical reaction that leaves the ink-receptive coating ready to be activated. The image can then be inked and transferred directly to paper or to an intermediary surface that will print the design.

The following processes are identified as relief, intaglio, planographic, etc., by the name in parentheses immediately following the process term.

Aquatint (intaglio): A design cut into a metal plate coated with rosin. When the plate is heated and submerged into an acid bath, the lines between the grains of rosin appear richly textured.

Chiaroscuro Woodcut (relief): A woodblock in which the key block is inked in layers of a translucent color or printed in graduated monochromatic tones on a colored paper to give the effect of a drawing or gouache.

Chine Appliqué (Chine Collé) (intaglio): A collage technique in which the image is impressed into a thin sheet of China paper that has been glued to a stronger, thicker sheet and printed simultaneously.

Chromolithograph (planographic): The artist draws the design onto a prepared zinc plate that is cut mechanically from a transfer plate. Colors are then sep-

Aquatint:
French Family Dancing by Rowlandson. 18th century. Lyons Ltd.

Chiaroscuro: *Proserpine* by Goltzius. 16th century. Lyons Ltd.

arated by eye and inked on a series of plates with an aniline oil based ink. Colors can overlap, producing the shading and rich velvety tones of oil painting, which made this a favorite process of the Victorians.

Cliché Verre (intaglio): The artist scratches the design onto a glass plate that has been covered with paint. When a photosensitive paper is placed underneath and the plate exposed to light, the image prints to the paper.

Collograph or Collotype (combination relief and intaglio): Begun in the 1880s, this process builds up the printing surface on a plate by applying various photosensitive, gelatin-like materials and then the design is mechanically cut into that substance. The plate is then submerged into an acid bath that erodes the printing surface and as each area of the design reaches the desired depth, the plate is "stopped out" and the area blocked. The process is repeated until each area has reached the desired depth, with the darkest tones being those longest in the acid. The

plate is inked and printed, producing a print that looks very much like a watercolor painting.

Digital or Computer Graphics (mechanical): The artist inputs his design into the computer, (which becomes the medium), with a stylus, plotter, or mouse and views the imagery in progress on a screen. When he is satisfied he chooses a computer-compatible printer that will produce the effect he desires. Dot matrix prints lines with small pin heads of ink; ink jets spray the ink to form continuous lines; laser printers transfer colors and lines by heat and pressure; Xerox prints with dust-like grains of ink; and even the fax machine can be used to print these digital designs. The image is then printed to the paper.

Drypoint Etching (intaglio): The design is cut by pulling various diamond-pointed tools across the metal plate. The depth of the line is controlled by the artist's muscular strength, skill, and experience. This method of cutting produces a rough ridge along the cut called a burr. It is this burr that gives the drypoint etching its characteristic silky and velvety soft tone rather than the clean edged lines of a typical etching or engraving.

Engraving (intaglio): Begun in the sixteenth century, an engraving is a design cut into a metal plate with an engraver's needle, which leaves recessed troughs

Chromolith-ograph:
Yosemite by Prang. 19th century. Lyons Ltd.

Collotype:
Gardens of Rome by Vignal. 20th century. Lyons Ltd.

**Etching &
Drypoint**:
Akt mit Facher
by Chagall.
20th century.
Lyons Trust.

Engraving:
*Batavian
Expedition to
China* by
Meursium.
17th century.
Lyons Ltd.

to hold ink. The levels of dimension and depth are provided by varying the depth of the cut. Shading is accomplished with a technique known as cross hatching (fine lines drawn close together and crossing over each other). Early engravers worked with copper plates which were replaced by steel in the mid-nineteenth century. Modern plates can be done on anything that you can cut into (glass, resins, plastic). The plate is inked and wiped clean and the dampened paper is forced into the cuts by the pressure of the printing press rolling over the plate, cranked by hand much like an old-fashioned clothes

Etching:
Arco di
Septimo Servo
for *Vedute de
Roma* by
Piranesi.
18th century.
Lyons Ltd.

wringer. Modern presses are run by vacuum or hydraulic pressure.

Etching (intaglio): In etching, the metal plate is coated with a varnish-like acid-resistant material called a "ground." The artist draws his design onto the ground with a burin (a sharp needle-like tool), which removes part of the ground. The plate is dipped in an acid bath and the incised drawing is etched (eaten away) by the action of the acid. The plate is then inked and wiped and run through a press like a clothes wringer. The parts of the copper plate that appear in the finished print as the black or colored area are the parts that the artist etched; the white areas are the parts left untouched.

Giclée (photomechanical): A reproductive process in which an oil painting, water color, drawing, or collage is copied either photographically or mechanically to the computer and digitally enhanced before being transferred to an Iris printer and published. The color management of the water-based ink produces a lustrous and continuous tone that is equal to or better than lithography or screen printing.

Linocut (relief): The artist draws the design on a linoleum block and carves away the open spaces. When the block is inked, only the raised portion prints. The process now often uses a rubber or layered cardboard surface. It is not suitable for detailed designs.

Linocut:
Morte d'Arthur by Beardsley. 19th century. Lyons Ltd.

Lithograph (planographic): The artist draws the design on a flat Bavarian limestone with a greasy crayon, or *tusche*. The stone is dampened with water and then inked. The ink clings to the tusche but not to the dampened areas. Since the design is neither raised above the surface nor cut into the stone, the quality of the impression is determined by the chemicals in the tusche that attract or reject the ink. The inked image is transferred when a piece of paper is pressed against the stone and run through a lithographic sliding press. The image may then be colored by hand, or the stone re-inked to print color. Lithographs are relatively inexpensive and can print an almost unlimited number of impressions. In modern lithography, the stone is often replaced with zinc or aluminum plates.

Metal Cut (relief): The design is drawn on a copper plate and the background cut away. The surface is textured with dots made from the delicate tools used by goldsmiths. The copper plate is mounted on a wood block so that it can be set into a frame with moveable pieces of type for printing. The plate is then inked and the design on the raised surface printed to the paper with pressure from a smooth object (like a stone) or by hand. Since the plates were small, often several plates would be joined together to form a sequential design, much like a comic strip.

Lithograph: *Le Dimanche au Jardin des Plantes* by Daumier. 19th century. Lyons Ltd.
Metal Cut: *Untitled Castle Scene* by Verard. 15th century. Lyons Ltd.
Mezzotint: *La Naissance d'Amour* by Haid. 18th century. Lyons Ltd.

Mezzotint (intaglio): This process first appeared in
the seventeenth century but still finds favor today.
The artist first textures the surface of the metal plate
with a series of spiked rocker balls (roulettes) which,
as they cut into the plate, produce a rough edge or

**Mixed Media
(lithograph,
offset and
collage):**
Picabia II by
Dine. 20th
century.
Lyons Trust.

Offset:
*Peter Pan in
Kensington
Gardens* by
Rackham.
20th century.
Lyons Ltd.

burr that holds small amounts of ink. The line of the design is then cut into the plate in the same way as an engraving. When the plate is inked and printed on paper the engraving produces the outline and the textured area produces the dark shading. Lighter shadings are produced by scraping and burnishing the surface to achieve contrasting shades, which print from dark to light. Mezzotints were and are still costly and labor-intensive. In the eighteenth century a copper plate could print only twenty or so copies. Today's mezzotints are done on steel but still can only produce roughly fifty prints.

Mixed Media (multiple processes): An artist creates a design with the intent of printing it in parts using various processes. Therefore a mixed media plate can be a composite of individual plates, resins, stones, blocks, or stencils, which are then printed sequentially on paper.

Offset (planographic): This developed as a variation of lithography. In an offset print, the artist's design can be drawn on a stone, a paper, or a photographic plate. The plate is placed in the bed of a horizontal printing press and instead of printing directly from stone to paper, the design is transferred to an intermediary metal cylinder covered with a rubber blanket. The roller then transfers the image to the paper. Letterpress and photo offset printing both evolved from this process.

Photo Engraving (intaglio): The artist's design is created from a photograph, painting, or drawing or a combination of both or multiple of both superimposed on each other. The design is transferred from these mediums by photography, creating a positive transparency film. The area that prints the image is opaque on the positive transparency and the area that is not to print is transparent.

Gravure (Photo Engraving): *Stage Set* by Craig. 20th century. Lyons Ltd.

The positive is placed on a photosensitive plate and developed like a photograph. There are many variants of this process: gravure, rotogravure, photogravure, and heliogravure are but a few.

Pochoir (stencil): A design made by the artist is analyzed mechanically and broken into color patterns for which individual color stencils are cut. The stencils, originally made of oiled paper, can now be made of plastic, copper, or brass. Color is applied by hand through the openings in the stencil and layering and shading can be added by overlaying additional stencils or by using different brushes.

Pochoir: *Anemone* by Foord. 20th century. Lyons Ltd.

Serigraph: *Stage Set for Macbeth* by Stern. 20th century. Lyons Ltd.
Silk Screen: *Germany, The Land of Music* by Von Axter. 20th century. Lyons Ltd.
Stipple Engraving: *Lady Mary Campbell* by Ramsay. 18th century. Lyons Ltd.

Serigraph or Silk Screening (stencil): In this twentieth-century adaptation of the stencil, the artist draws his design directly onto silk or a screen that has been stretched across a frame. Areas that are not to be printed are blocked out by filling up the mesh in the screen with a varnish-like substance. Color is pressed through the openings in the mesh onto the paper placed underneath. Later in the nineteenth century much of the printing was done by photo-processed stencils.

Soft Ground Etching (intaglio): While the technique is the same as in etching, the process and results are somewhat different. The metal plate is coated with a ground that never fully hardens. Textured patterns as well as the lines of the design can be cut into this softer ground so that, when the plate is exposed to the acid and inked, the resulting image will contain both. The end result is a softer, more delicate line that looks almost like a pencil drawing.

Stipple Engraving (intaglio): The artist lightly engraves the outline of his design on a copper plate and then uses a tool called a stippling burin to lay down thousands of minute dots within the engraved line. These dots of varying depths build up on the plate and create the effect of shaded colors or tones when printed.

Woodcut or Woodblock (relief): The design is drawn on a plank of wood and the area in between the drawn lines is cut away with a knife or gouge, leaving a printable image in raised relief. Alternatively, the image can be drawn on paper and glued down to the woodblock before cutting. Whether by itself or integrated into a frame with moveable typeset, the block is inked and pressed onto paper. Originally woodcuts were printed with a screw press or rubbed by hand pressure. Each print had to be processed individually—inked, inserted, screwed down, unscrewed, removed, and hung to dry. It was at best a tiresome and laborious process and produced somewhere between three hundred to five hundred images. Today's flatbed presses can be run by hand, but many are automated. Woodblocks can be colored by hand or printed in color. Those printed in color can be done either by blocking out areas and re-inking color by color, or with successive blocks done for each color needed. The ability to print color within the lines of the design on the matrix block is called registration, and the ability to keep the color inside the lines is very important.

Woodcut:
Untitled Battle Scene for Brabant Chronicle. 15th century. Lyons Ltd.

Wood Engraving: *The Leopard* by Bewick. 18th century. Lyons Ltd.

Wood Engraving (intaglio): The artist draws the design either directly onto the wood block or onto paper that would then be pasted to the wood block. The image is cut into the wood against the grain, inked, and printed onto paper with a roller press. Cutting against the grain produces a block that can print as many as 900,000 images.

WHAT TERMS SHOULD I KNOW?

1. What is a "state" and why is it important?

An artist may "pull" (print) an image as many times as he wishes in his lifetime. In each pull of the plate there is something that differentiates that impression from the previous one—a change in the imagery or a different kind of paper. Each printing is called a state. States of antique prints are usually identified in lowercase Roman numerals (ii/vi). Modern graphics use Arabic numerals (2/5).

While the basic image in a particular print remains the same from impression to impression, each printing does produce a unique object because of differences in inking, pressure, the dampness of the paper, and the gradual deterioration of the printing surface. Often the differences are minute, but there are times when they are dramatic. The different impressions that are produced by each of these changes are called the different states of the print. In other words, a state is an alteration or variation of image or the paper on which it is printed within a lifetime edition. Generally, though not always, an earlier state of an etching or engraving is more valuable than a later one because the plate produces a clearer image in the first stages of the printing process. Descriptions of fine prints will frequently refer to them as "first state," "second state," and so on. This numerical description should not be confused with the modern convention of numbering impressions in pencil on the print itself. The characteristics of each state can be determined by using a reference book called a "catalogue raisonné."

2. What is a catalogue raisonné?

Serious research begins by consulting reference books. A catalogue raisonné is a listing and description of all the works of a given artist, listing states, editions, and in some cases, later copies and forgeries. Almost every major artist has a scholarly study of his work that uses reference numbers to identify the amount of editions published, the size of each edition, the paper used, and whatever changes in the imagery that may have occurred.

3. What does signing and numbering signify?

Early prints were not signed and were often done entirely anonymously. When signatures first began to appear they were done directly on the plate and printed within the image, often with just initials (for example, Albrecht Dürer's famous AD). By the end of the eighteenth century, when artists no longer carved and printed their own plates, we begin to see, below the image itself, the artist's name printed on the left and the engraver or lithographer's name printed on the right.

Late in the nineteenth century, as the size and quality of prints became increasingly unpredictable, artists began the convention of signing prints in pencil to indicate that they were authorized, inspected, and approved by the artist himself. That signature was meant to verify the authenticity and originality of the design and the quality of that impression. Abuses of this procedure—for example, Salvador Dalí signed blank sheets of paper for his publisher even before they were printed—led to the convention of numbering each authorized print to document which print a given image was in a particular sequence.

This in itself is somewhat deceptive because the same graphic can be printed in subsequent editions with a similar set of numbers. For example, I have an original Picasso aquatint that is signed in pencil and numbered 10/300, indicating that it is the tenth print of an edition of three hundred copies. You would assume that this means that there were a total of only three hundred copies printed. However, in the catalogue raisonné for Picasso you will find that there are five additional signed and numbered editions of three hundred prints each done in his lifetime, each looking exactly the same but printed on different kinds of paper at different times. That means my Picasso is really one of fifteen hundred pulls of that particular plate.

Limited edition prints can also be found in books and portfolios. Sometimes the prints are individually signed and numbered. More commonly the title page will indicate that this is copy number *xx* of an edition of *xxxx* privately printed copies. One should think twice before separating a book or portfolio that is in good condition. There is far more value to the whole than the parts and, once a book or portfolio is separated, there will be little left for future generations to enjoy.

Today we are faced with another problem: Reproductive color "prints" are appearing on the market, often sanctioned by the artists themselves. Photomechanical prints are *not* original prints, even if signed and/or numbered. Today, there are a few artists who are actively involved in producing images by intervening and altering the design as it is being produced (much like some disc jockeys who produce a new sound by manually rotating a record while it is playing). However, even with the artist's involvement, it is uncertain how these prints will fare over time when compared with original prints. Their aesthetic and monetary value is questionable.

4. What is a proof?

A proof is a pull of the plate that is done at varying times by the artist to ascertain whether the plate he is working on is printing as he intended. There are several kinds of proofs that can be done before the artist issues the first print for sale. The first proofs will be "trial proofs"—proofs that check the placement, color, and clarity of the image. These prints are numbered like the regular edition except that the numbers are done in lower case roman numerals (for example ii/vi). The final proof is signed "*bon à tirer*" (good to pull) or, in the United States, "R.T.P" (right to print), indications that the artist is satisfied and the printer can begin. Artist's proofs are that small portion of the edition that the artist keeps for himself and are marked "A/P" (artist's proof). Often the artist will make notes or sketches in the margins of a proof. These drawings themselves are called a "remarque," and the proof itself is identified as a "remarqued proof." The final proof of the plate is the cancellation proof, which is printed to show that the plate has been slashed or defaced enough that no further images can be pulled from it. There are many other kinds of proofs, but these are the most significant. Proofs, because of their rarity, often command higher prices in the marketplace than regular editions. ◼

2

A BRIEF HISTORY OF GRAPHIC ARTS

While it is often assumed that prints originated with the invention of the printing press in fifteenth-century Europe, in truth the history of printing goes back to the earliest civilizations. The first prints occurred when beautifully carved signature seals were stamped on vellum or papyrus in ancient Mesopotamia around 3500 B.C. Later, across the Mediterranean Sea the Greeks experimented with forms that stamped coins, while still later the Romans replaced their signature seals with stencils. Remember the "Five P's" from our prints primer in chapter one? What follows is a brief history of how **paper**, **presses**, **processes**, **people**, and **periods** as they relate to prints developed individually and simultaneously.

IN THE BEGINNING . . .

The invention of **paper** was the first step in the explosion of knowledge that was to mark the coming centuries. We first learn of paper and papermaking in a chronicle of the Han dynasty in China in 105 A.D. The chronicle tells of the work of Ts'ai Lun, who developed a method of beating rags, tree bark, and hemp waste in a stone mortar, producing a surface suitable for writing and painting. The process became a closely guarded secret that was protected by successive Chinese emperors and remained virtually unchanged. The Chinese had a culture rich in verbal and visual imagery, and its influence spread throughout Asia; knowledge of papermaking would not reach Europe until the late Middle Ages.

Eventually paper found its way to the West along the caravan routes, such as the Silk Road through central Asia. The knowledge of how paper was made did not appear until the eighth century, when an Arab governor discovered two Chinese papermakers among his prisoners and used them to establish a paper mill in the Central Asian city of Samarkand, in present-day Uzbekistan, in 751 A.D. In the eighth century, while most of Europe was still submerged in the dark ages, Frankish emperor Charlemagne (742–814) discovered paper during his quest to conquer the influence of the Middle East in Spain. Upon his return from Spain, where he had been introduced to the Moorish papermakers, he issued a Directive on the Study of Letters that included the opening of schools to all children, the correct copying of important historical manuscripts, and the adoption, for the spoken and written word, of the old Roman alphabet, which subsequently brought literacy back to the western world.

Although there is evidence that there were experiments in printing books in China during the T'ang dynasty (618–906 A.D.), the earliest dated illustrated book was found relatively recently. The Diamond Sutra (868 A.D.) was found in 1907 in a cave in Chinese Turkistan, and its carved relief woodcuts are richly and skillfully detailed. Like many of its predecessors, it was part of the spreading of the Buddhist culture across Asia but, because it and thousands of other scrolls were hidden in a sealed cave during the Mongol invasions of the late ninth century, the scrolls survived the ravages of time. After the departure of the Mongols in the tenth century, the subject matter of these books and scrolls expanded to include other needs and interests like botany, literature, and history. The earliest attempts at copperplate engravings are reported at the same time, but because of the difficulties encountered, this technique seems to have died out shortly thereafter.

The Arabs guarded the secret of paper making as carefully as had the Chinese, but paper was eventually introduced into Europe following the Moorish invasion (711) and conquest of the region of Andalusia (al-Andalus) in southern Spain. Papermaking factories were flourishing in Toledo by the mid-twelfth century and had reached France and Germany by the fourteenth century.

All of the limited attempts at disseminating knowledge through handwritten illuminated or printed block books were overshadowed by the work of Johannes Gutenberg (c. 1398–1468) in Mainz, Germany, in the mid-fifteenth century. His invention of a matrix frame, which could hold an image as well as a large number of moveable type pieces at one time, allowed multiple volumes to be crafted and printed at an unprecedented rate so that the printing of books became a major cultural force in the fifteenth century. Suddenly printing **presses** were at work everywhere in Germany, the Netherlands, France, Italy, and England, producing an explosion of knowledge that helped move the world from the limitations of the Middle Ages into the flowering of learning and artistic achievement known as the Renaissance.

Most antique graphics were created to serve as a vehicle of communication or education. While artists were commissioned to paint for an individual patron of the wealthy class, the graphic illustrators had to please a general audience. The artist's mission was to educate, enlighten, and entertain both those who could read and those who could not. A picture truly was "worth a thousand words."

THE FIFTEENTH CENTURY: GOTHIC IMAGERY

The earliest prints to appear in the fifteenth century were primitive metalcuts done in a relief process. The illustrations were done in strips and often joined together to produce a larger design, much like today's comic strips. The **process** was laborious and produced only a few images at a time—not a problem since there were only a few people who could afford them!

The woodcut, also a relief technique, quickly replaced the metalcut when it was discovered that it could be placed into a matrix along with moveable type and printed in larger quantities. Most of the early artists working in this medium were anonymous or identified simply by monograms. Others are names we now recognize—for example, Albrecht Dürer, Hendrik Goltzius, and Hans Holbein—as milestones in the development of graphic art.

One of the best examples of the woodcut process is Hartmann Schedel's *Nuremberg Chronicle*. Printed in 1493 in an edition of eleven hundred copies, the *Chronicle* is a pictorial history of man and his accomplishments beginning with Adam and Eve and continuing through the Old and New Testaments, classical and medieval history, and ending with the world of the fifteenth century. The woodcut illustrations depicted all the important people and places in this time span, some eighteen hundred titles. However, the 645 repeated illustrations are iconographic and merely represent the figures depicted. In that time of limited travel and knowledge, who would have known whether a portrait was actually one of Constantine or Charlemagne? While the gothic views of the world seem distorted to us now, in its time the *Nuremberg Chronicle* was truly a monumental undertaking.

THE SIXTEENTH CENTURY: MANNERISM

In the sixteenth century the developing economic power of the merchant classes and the expanding world of such maritime explorers as Christopher Columbus and Ferdinand Magellan created a demand for a more accurate and realistic vision of man and his world. The introduction of vanishing point perspective and the camera obscura added depth

Tilling the Fields for Virgil's *Georgics* by unknown artist.
Woodcut.
16th century.
Lyons Ltd.

Pisa for *Nuremberg Chronicle* by Wolgemuth.
Woodcut.
15th century.
Lyons Ltd.

and detail to the prints that documented current events. The influence of Michelangelo Buonarroti and Leonardo da Vinci, artists who had learned to combine art with scientific inquiry, produced ever more elegant and realistic portraits and religious scenes. A new, more sensual and elegantly detailed style appeared at the same time, and this exaggerated style came to be known as **Mannerism** (about 1520–90). A more refined version of the woodcut known as *chiaroscuro* (from Italian, meaning bright and dark) captured in monochromatic tones the elegance and detail of the period.

The invention of engraving, an intaglio process, provided a more sophisticated and detailed print early in the sixteenth century. The styles of the early engravers varied from dense and heavy to light and lyrical. Like the early woodcut artists, the first engravers were primarily identified by their monograms. Many of them worked in several mediums with equal skill. One of the first artists to work on both the canvas and the copper plate was the German Albrecht Dürer (1471–1528). His early work is first found in the gothic imagery of the *Nuremberg Chronicle*. After traveling to Italy and learning vanishing point perspective, his work in both woodcut and engraving became a dramatic elaboration on whatever theme he was exploring. His prints were addressed not just to patrons but also to the man in the street, and his images of the passion of Christ were as dramatic, shocking, and powerful as today's movie portrayals. It should be noted that many of his plates are still in existence today, so it is important to check the paper and inks of any particular impression. Dürer set the standard for two generations of master printmakers such as Albrecht Altdorfer, Hans Sebald Beham, Lucas Cranach, Hans Holbein, and Pieter Brueghel, who carried the process of engraving successfully through the sixteenth century and into the seventeenth.

Very shortly, a more sophisticated variation of the engraving technique appeared. With etching, also an intaglio technique, it is possible to achieve more contrast and depth and incredible detail. Etching, however, requires much skill and experience since mistakes are almost impossible to correct. Drypoint etchings have a characteristically velvety soft tone, rather than the clean-edged lines of a typical etching or engraving. Soft ground etchings make it possible to add texture to the plate. By the seventeenth century, most prints combined engraving and some form of etching in a single plate and the less sophisticated line engravings began to disappear.

THE SEVENTEENTH CENTURY: BAROQUE

The master engravers of the seventeenth century, both major and minor, explored the virtual and allegorical landscape with zeal, and their images reached an ever-widening audience. People were intrigued by the humanism, fed by a revival of classical learning, that showed the importance of mankind in a realistic environment surrounded by objects of everyday life. This harmony of man and nature was symbolized in a style known as **baroque** (fl. 1590–1725), which used rich colors, exaggerated shapes, and contrasts in shadow and light to document subjects from plants and portraits to architecture and allegory. It was a period of monumental art. The Dutch painter Rembrandt van Rijn (1606–1669) is, of course, unmatched in skill and technique, but the portraits and scenes of Peter Paul Rubens, Wenzel Hollar, Jacques Callot, and Claude Lorrain; the botanicals of Emanuel Sweert; the maps of Abraham

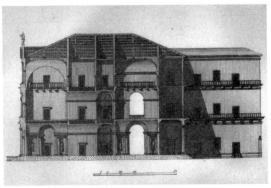

Bust of Man Wearing a High Cap by **Rembrandt.** Etching. 17th century. Lyons Ltd.
Daffodils for *Florilegium* **by Sweert.** Engraving. 17th century. Lyons Ltd.
Butterflies & Lemons for *Insectorium Surinamensis.* Engraving.
17th century. Lyons Ltd.
Teatro Olympico for *Quattro Libri* **by Scamozzi.** Engraving. 18th century. Lyons Ltd.

Ortelius and John Speed; and the architecture of Andrea Palladio were also important and provided images that made the world more accessible to those who had the time and money to view them.

Working at the same time as Rembrandt, the apothecary Basil Besler was commissioned by the Bishop-Prince of Nuremberg to document all his extensive gardens,

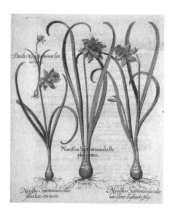

Narcissus for *Hortus Eystettensis* **by Besler.** Engraving. 17th century. Lyons Ltd.

which contained specimens of plants from all over the then known world. His elegant engravings depict plants that were needed for culinary, medicinal, and domestic purposes. Published in 1613 in an edition of three hundred copies (only a few of which were hand-colored), *Hortus Eystettensis* was the first herbal of the Renaissance. The gardens were destroyed in 1633 during the Thirty Years' War (1618–1648). First editions are on a heavy paper with text on the back of each sheet. Second editions rework the plates, removing the text, and are on a lighter paper. A third edition commissioned by the heirs in 1713 to celebrate the centennial anniversary is basically a restrike, as is a fourth printing in 1750. Both of these later editions are printed from worn plates on inferior paper. The copper plates were melted down in 1817.

THE EIGHTEENTH CENTURY: ROCOCO AND NEOCLASSICISM

The eighteenth century was an age of upheaval and movement in every aspect of life: artistic, social, political, technical, and economic. Two styles of imagery flourished side by side. Rococo prints sought to elaborate on the lives of the rich and powerful in an almost dreamy and sometimes melancholy world. Neoclassical prints sought to return to the knowledge and enlightenment of ancient civilizations (particularly that of the Greeks) in order to define reality.

Just as printing processes had undergone major changes in the seventeenth century, papermaking made great advances in the eighteenth century. The new papers were lighter in weight and finer in texture than their earlier counterparts, undergoing a much more complicated production process that resulted in a surface better suited to receive the more intricate, delicate and detailed etchings and engravings of the **rococo** period (about 1715–50). We are fortunate that Denis Diderot (1713–1784) provided a detailed analysis of contemporary papermaking in his *Encyclopedia*, published in Paris beginning in 1751. The complicated and laborious process of papermaking began by gathering rags that were then sorted, cut into strips, and rolled into balls. The balls were soaked in water and lye and allowed to stand and ferment for weeks. The portion not destroyed by the fermentation process was skimmed off and placed in another vat in a proportion of thirty percent rag to seventy percent water. The mixture was then pounded with a water-driven hammer until the remaining fibers were thoroughly dissolved. Then the vat man dipped his mold into the mix, let excess water run off, and shook the frame back and forth to distribute the pulp evenly on a screen, thus obtaining the desired thickness.

Two kinds of molds were in use at the time. One crossed strips of wire at right angles and produced a *laid* paper with clearly visible screen marks. Refinements in printing techniques led to *wove* paper, which was formed on a mesh screen and produced a smooth surface without the laid lines. A design or maker's mark made of wire was attached to the mold, producing an imprint known as the *water mark* as the paper dried. A frame called a *deckle* fitted over the mold to prevent the pulp from running off. When pulp ran under the edge of the deckle, it produced an uneven edge and this *deckle edge* became a characteristic of fine handmade papers.

The screen was then passed to the coucher who removed each sheet of paper and placed it on a wool felt blotter while the vat man returned to dip a second sheet. After a large enough stack of sheets had accumulated, they were weighted, squeezed flat and partially dried in a hand press by a layman, then hung in groups of five to finish drying. If a fine finish was desired, the paper was finished by glazing (smoothing the surface with a stone or mechanical roller) or sizing (coating with starch or animal glue to close the minute spaces between the fibers). Diderot, in his attempt to survey all scientific and industrial knowledge, exposed the intensive use of human labor involved in each industry. His project (co-edited with Jean Le Rond d'Alembert), a monument of the Enlightenment, caused great controversy and was seen as a radical threat to convention and orthodoxy. As a result of his efforts to document his age, he suffered twenty years of abuse and harassment.

The eighteenth century also saw important changes in the production of prints. Earlier graphic processes were refined and embellished to better accommodate the elaborate details and lavish proportions of the rococo period. The increasing expense of hand coloring drove artists and publishers to explore new ways of producing color images. Several variations of traditional relief and intaglio processes emerged as a solution. The mezzotint, an intaglio process that first appeared at the end of the seventeenth century, found favor because the images replicated the rich tones of watercolors or drawings. The aquatint (also an intaglio process) was usually done in combination with line engraving and produced the effect of a watercolor painting but without the shading and brush strokes. The plates were usually inked in three flat colors and then finished with additional hand coloring under the artist's direction to complete the effect. The stipple engraving (another intaglio process), with its pattern of minute dots of differing depths, created the effect of richly shaded colors or tones.

The eighteenth century was also a time of artistic giants. In England, William Hogarth, James Gillray, and Thomas Rowlandson explored the foibles of eighteenth-century society in satirical prints, while in France, François Boucher, Jean-Honoré Fragonard, and Antoine Watteau pursued whimsical and allegorical themes.

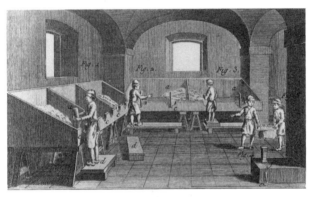

Papermaking: Sorting Rags, *Encyclopedia* by Diderot. Engraving. 18th century.
Lyons Ltd.
Papermaking: Cutting Rags, *Encyclopedia* by Diderot. Engraving. 18th century.
Lyons Ltd.
Papermaking: Papermaking: Washing and Bleaching Rags, *Encyclopedia* by Diderot.
Engraving. 18th century. Lyons Ltd.

Papermaking: Molding and Processing, *Encyclopedia* by Diderot. Engraving. 18th century. Lyons Ltd.
Papermaking: Polishing and Folding, *Encyclopedia* by Diderot. Engraving. 18th century. Lyons Ltd.
Papermaking: Cutting Paper, *Encyclopedia* by Diderot. Engraving. 18th century. Lyons Ltd.

***The Election*
by Hogarth.**
Engraving.
18th century.
Lyons Ltd.

***Les Enfants
de Bacchus*
by Watteau.**
Etching.
18th century.
Lyons Ltd.

The frontiers of the New World were expanding each day, and everybody waited breathlessly for prints that would show them some aspect of life in these distant places. Maps did exactly that and were highly prized as each new edition was printed. One of the most interesting conventions in mapmaking was the practice of drawing California as an island. Between 1622 and 1751, two hundred forty-nine maps, from miniatures to double pages, were drawn this way. Mariners knew the eastern and southern coasts of the Americas in great

detail, but the West was totally unexplored. The Peter Schenk map of the world not only shows the island of California and the unexplored Pacific Northwest but also the mythical land bridge across the Bering Strait connecting America to Asia (which is supposedly how America was first populated). Detailed descriptions of what these explorers had found were much sought after. François Martinet portrayed the birds of the New World while Johann Weinmann detailed the flowers then known in Europe. John Weber, who documented Captain Cook's third voyage that discovered the Hawaiian Islands, recorded the natives and their customs, while Mark Catesby concentrated on the flora and fauna of Georgia and the Carolinas.

Diverse Orbis Terre by **Schenk.** Engraving. 18th century. Lyons Ltd.

In Japan, color woodblocks, which first appeared in the seventeenth century, flourished. Kitagawa Utamaro, Hishikawa Moronobu, the elder Toyokuni, Toshusai Sharaku, and Suzuki Harunobu, with their stylized figures and delicately colored kimonos and landscapes, depicted a Japan untouched by time or outside influences.

In Italy, one artist above all stood out. Giovanni Battista (also Giambattista) Piranesi (1720–1778),

Manakin Birds by Martinet. Engraving. 18th century. Lyons Ltd.
Tulips for *Phantanthoza Iconographia* **by Weinmann.** Mezzotint. 18th century.
Lyons Ltd.
Night Dance in Hapaee for *Capt. Cooke's Third Voyage* **by Weber.** Engraving. 18th
century. Lyons Ltd.
Paris Bird for *Natural History of Georgia & the Carolina's* **by Catesby.** Engraving. 18th
century. Lyons Ltd.
Bust of Two Geisha **by Utamaro. Woodblock.** 18th century. Lyons Ltd.

known as the Rembrandt of architecture, worked relentlessly to document the glories of ancient Rome. His famous views (*Vedute di Roma*) contributed greatly to the development of Neoclassicism while stimulating interest in preserving the archaeological ruins of the city. After the fall of the Roman Empire (ca. fifth century A.D.), Rome itself had deteriorated into a provincial city with the remnants of the ancient city in total decay. The Forum was under 18 feet of mud with only the tops of arches and columns showing, and Romanesque and Renaissance buildings had incorporated other ruins into their structures. The Colosseum was a tenement with gypsies living inside (in Piranesi's engraving you can see salamis and clothes hanging in the arches of the building). These large-scale etchings were circulated throughout Europe and had a profound influence on the architecture of Robert Adam in England. The states and editions of the *Vedute* done in Piranesi's lifetime are well documented, but restrikes abound. His son inherited the plates and, adding an Arabic numeral to the upper right-hand corner, restruck them in Paris in 1810 (the Paris edition). The family then sold the plates to the Vatican library in 1823, and bearing the imprint of the Calcographia, they have been restruck annually in increasingly inferior editions.

THE NINETEENTH CENTURY: ROMANTICISM AND IMPRESSIONISM

The nineteenth century saw a multiplicity of styles, a refinement of earlier processes and an awareness of the need to find a less expensive and time-consuming way to provide prints for an ever-expanding market. The harsh realities of life after a half century of wars brought an end to the rococo period. As Neoclassicism, driven by more far-reaching travel and new archeological discoveries, continued well into the nineteenth century, two different artistic styles began to emerge. **Neoclassicism** (ca. 1750 to 1850) sought to return to the knowledge and enlightenment of ancient civilizations (particularly that of the Greeks) in order to define reality. **Romanticism** (ca. 1789 to late 1800s) sought to avoid confronting the realities of life through emotional and imaginative imagery. These styles functioned side by side throughout most of the nineteenth century.

Neoclassical artist John Flaxman, whose line engravings catalogued the classical Greek vases unearthed by Lord Elgin, powerfully illustrated the tragedies of Aeschylus and later became Wedgwood's major classical ceramic designer. The neoclassical architectural masterpieces of Robert Adam of Scotland and Thomas Jefferson were carefully and classically documented with detailed engravings of floor plans and elevations. At the same time William Blake's romantic and dramatic engravings of the *Book of Job*, Robert Thornton's larger-than-life abstract and mystical botanical images, J. J. Grandville's (Jean Ignace Isidore Gérard) *Les Fleurs Animées*, with flowers depicted as languid women, Eugène Delacroix's allegorical etchings of historical events, and Francisco Goya's tormented etchings of the disasters of war were part of the Romantic movement that attempted to improve the world by rebelling against the old corrupt conventions of society.

In the mid-nineteenth century, a series of inventions began a chain of events that forever changed the processes of printing and marketing prints. In the late eighteenth century, the first successful papermaking machine had been invented. A web machine of continuous woven mesh, it could turn out great quantities of paper without the need for any human labor. The demand for useable paper became overwhelming almost overnight, as the Industrial Revolution, with its rapidly developing middle class and its accompanying science and technology, strained to produce the images demanded by the public. Wood pulp, synthetic fibers, chemical bleaches, and additives replaced hemp, flax, and linen and forever changed both the craft and characteristics of paper and papermaking.

Old printing processes continued to find new uses, and new printing processes were added to the graphic lexicon, all of which made larger editions possible and graphics more accessible to a thirsty public. Engravings previously done on soft copper and laboriously run through a hand-cranked press could produce only minimal editions. The introduc-

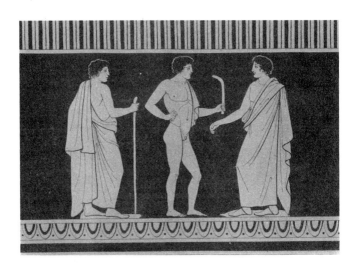

Greek Vase Fragments for *Hamilton's Antiquities* by Flaxman.
Engraving.
19th century.
Lyons Ltd.

L'Orangier Lady for *Les Fleurs Animées* by Grandville.
Lithograph.
19th century.
Lyons Ltd.

tion of indestructible steel plates and a steam press that could run night and day produced such large-sized editions at such reasonable costs that graphic art became readily available to everyone. Thousands of views of the landscapes and cities of Europe, America, the Orient, and the Middle East were produced by artists like William Bartlett, Thomas Allom,

Imperial Palace for *Manners & Customs of China* by Allom. Engraving. 19th century.
Lyons Ltd.
Slenidera Gould Toucan for *Monograph on Toucans* by Gould. Lithograph.
19th century. Lyons Ltd.
***Wild Flowers* by Loudon.** Lithograph. 19th century. Lyons Ltd.
Northern Hare for *Quadrupeds of North America* by Audubon. Lithograph.
19th century. Lyons Ltd.

***Chippewa Squaw* by McKenny & Hall.** Lithograph. 19th century. Lyons Ltd.

***One Hundred Views of Provinces* by Hiroshige.** Woodblock. 19th century. Lyons Ltd.

***Geisha with Umbrella* by Toyokuni III.** Woodblock. 19th century. Lyons Ltd.

and J.M.W. Turner for a public thirsty for illustrations of faraway places. The documentation of plant, animal, and bird species as well as indigenous peoples were executed in variations of the intaglio process in engravings by artists like Alexander Wilson, John

Un Seigneur du Temps de François 1 by Delacroix. Etching and drypoint. 19th century. Lyons Trust.

Les Gitanos by Manet. Etching. 19th century. Lyons Trust.

James Audubon, John Gould, William Curtis, Pierre-Joseph Redouté, and Carl Bodmer.

In Japan the art of the woodblock continued to flourish. Depictions of important personages, places, events, and folklore circulated through all levels of society. Known as *Ukiyo-e*, these subtle and complex images of the "floating world" were masterfully illustrated by numerous artists, among whom Katsushika Hokusai, Utagawa Kunisada (also known as Toyokuni III), and Ando Hiroshige were the best. After Admiral Perry's expedition in the early 1850s opened Japan to the western world, many of the late nineteenth-century European artists were influenced by the brightly colored abstract designs in these Japanese prints. Conversely, Japanese prints begin to reflect the new exposure to the culture and technology of Europe and America.

The invention of lithography revolutionized print making. This process proved to be inexpensive and could produce an almost unlimited number of impressions. As the medium developed, so did the skill of the artisans using the process. Among the early artists employing this new method were Honoré Daumier, John Gould, Carle Vernet, Eugène Delacroix, Francisco Goya, and Paul Gavarni, and in subsequent years Pierre-Auguste Renoir, Édouard Manet, Edgar Degas, Henri de Toulouse-Lautrec, and James McNeill Whistler.

One of the most prolific of the nineteenth-century lithographers was the firm of Currier and Ives, who documented American history, scenery, and people in what has become known as "cottage art." Their brightly colored lithographs depicting American life were printed in three different sizes and sold door to door from pushcarts for prices ranging from fifteen cents to three dollars and fifty cents (the latter, large folio prints now command several thousand dollars each). The large folio lithographs were carefully hand-colored. The small lithographs were hand-colored by stencil (one person did red, then passed it to the next person, who did green, etc.), and often colors fell outside the outlines.

The Pursuit **by Currier & Ives.** Lithograph. 19th century. Lyons Ltd.

At the same time, wood-engraved prints were revolutionizing journalism, producing numerous illustrations in the popular presses that recorded and influenced everyday life and politics. Building on the work of Thomas Bewick, publishers of the new popular illustrated periodicals like *Harper's Weekly* and the *Illustrated London News* discovered that with wood engravings they could print and distribute a significantly larger number of papers (up to 900,000 impressions could be pulled from a single block).

The artist and satirist Thomas Nast (1840–1902) single-handedly brought down New York's William Marcy "Boss" Tweed and his Tammany Hall political machine with his satiric cartoons. The capture of

The Tichborne Trial for Harper's Weekly. Wood Engraving. 19th century. Lyons Ltd.

"Saved by the skin of…" for *Harper's Weekly* by Nast. Wood Engraving. 19th century. Lyons Ltd.

Tweed, who had fled to Europe to escape prosecution, is credited to recognition based on Nast's cartoons that had been carried in the European press. Nast, known as America's iconographer, is the artist who created the image of the donkey to represent the Democratic Party and the elephant to represent the Republican Party. He transformed Santa Claus from the thin European Kris Kringle image to the jolly rotund figure that we now see everywhere. His biting cartoons ensured the defeat of presidential candidate Horace Greeley in the 1872 election against Ulysses S. Grant and documented the mistreatment in the United States of African Americans, Chinese, and Native Americans.

It was only a short leap from cottage art to poster art that lured viewers from everyday activities into the possibilities of a more exciting world. Large and colorful images inspired the man in the street to try new activities, travel to new places, and buy new products. Henri de Toulouse-Lautrec is credited with moving lithography in this new direction with his colorful and animated figures that drew you along with him

into the dance hall or bistro. Discovering that this form of advertising was both effective and collectible, opera performances, travel possibilities, and commercial products were soon immortalized in this dramatic and oversized art form.

Panurge by **Leander.** Lithograph. 20th century. Lyons Ltd.

The invention and subsequent production of the camera and its ability to reproduce images mechanically changed forever the nature of graphic arts. By the 1870s, photo-mechanical reproduction began to replace wood engraving and lithography as the principal medium of illustration. Chromolithography, collographs and collotypes, gravure and rotogravure, and offset all indicate a combination of mechanical and hand-done printing processes.

Souvenir d'Italie by **Corot.** Etching. 19th century. Lyons Trust.

The advent of the camera introduced a more realistic and less artificial view of people and nature, and the prints of the **Barbizon school** reflected this. J. B. Corot, Jean-François Millet, and Théodore Rousseau reflected on a simpler life and a desire to return to nature in their monochromatic engravings. At the same time a wildly different approach to art, reflecting the political and industrial upheavals that had marked the nineteenth century, exploded in vivid colors onto the art scene.

Impressionism, reflecting the political, technological, sociological, and economic turmoil of the last half of the nineteenth century, sought to rebel against the established art world and capture the interests

Femme Nue
Couche by
Renoir.
Etching.
20th century.
Lyons Trust.

and imagination of the public with new colors, subjects, and forms. Experimenting with a variety of different approaches to printed imagery, Impressionism used the newly developing theories of color as a reflection of emotion to capture both the vibrant mood of the people and the landscape surrounding them. In 1863, a group of artists whose work had been rejected for that year's French Academy exhibition put on an alternative, nonofficial exhibit called the *Salon des Refusés* (the exhibit of those refused). Impressionist "peintres-graveurs" (painters-engravers) such as Édouard Manet, Pierre-Auguste Renoir, Claude Monet, Camille Pissarro, Mary Cassatt, and Edgar Degas were intrigued by the contrasts and textures of color etching and lithography, tending their efforts toward more naturalistic images.

Influenced by Impressionism, the **Post-Impressionists** retained their love of color and light but began to move toward more formal compositions and recognizable shapes. With the influx of Japanese woodblock prints, Paul Cézanne, Georges Seurat, Paul Gauguin, and Vincent van Gogh were so compelled by their clear and bright colors that they began to paint outside of their studios *en pleine air* (in open air). The movement spread quickly and found favor with such American artists as Frederick Remington, Thomas Hill, Albert Bierstadt, and Thomas Moran as they documented the American landscape.

Grand Canyon of Arizona after **Moran.** Chromolithograph. 20th century. Lyons Ltd.

Portrait du Peintre A. Guillaumin Pendu by **Cézanne.** Etching. 19th century. Lyons Trust.

By the end of the nineteenth century the interest in collecting prints was flagging. Too many artists were producing too many prints in too many editions. The comfortable and predictable Victorians vacillated between the **Neo-Realistic** imagery of Winslow Homer, Seymour Haden, Camille Pissarro, and James McNeill Whistler and the lyrical and romantic

imagery of Aubrey Beardsley, Alphonse Mucha, William Bradley, Aristide Maillol, Pierre Bonnard, Gustav Klimt, Walter Crane, and Arthur Rackham. **Art Nouveau** (literally, "new art") was a style that originated in the 1890s and flourished until World War I (1914–1918). Characterized by flowing lines, elegant curves, asymmetry, and flower and leaf motifs, it paralleled the Arts and Crafts movement in the decorative arts.

Doorway and Vines by **Whistler.**
Etching.
19th century.
Lyons Trust.

The Kiss by **Behrens.**
Woodcut.
19th century.
Lyons Trust.

Der Polster by **Kurzweil.**
Woodcut.
20th century.
Lyons Trust.

Meanwhile a group of new young artists was moving away from what had been revolutionary art only a few decades earlier and toward more abstract imagery in which fragmented shapes and extended colors conveyed their intended message. This movement, which would later become known as **Art Deco**, incorporated geometric forms and sharp corners into art, architecture, furniture, and fashion in reaction to the flowing lines and delicate curves of the Art Nouveau period. (The name art deco comes from the Exposition Internationale des Arts Décoratifs et Industriels Modernes in Paris, 1925, originally planned for 1915 but postponed because of World War I.)

THE TWENTIETH CENTURY: ALL THE "-ISMS"

Pablo Picasso, Henri Matisse, and Georges Braque truly were the founders of what we today call **Modern Art**. It was the famous (or infamous) Armory Show of 1913 in New York that exposed the excitement of the avant-garde artists to the American art scene and to the world in general. The various "isms" that were yet to come were a reflection of these new styles and techniques.

Odalisque by Matisse. Lithograph. 20th century. Lyons Trust.

Le Faune by Picasso. Aquatint. 20th century. Lyons Trust.

Because this book is not an art history text, we will move fairly quickly through some of the more important modern movements. Remember that these movements were not sequential, but could and did run simultaneously, often overlapping. **Fauvism**, from the French word *fauve*, meaning "wild beast," was a term used to describe the early works of Henri Rousseau, Paul Gauguin, and Henri Matisse. Their prints not only were done with broad splashes of bright colors but

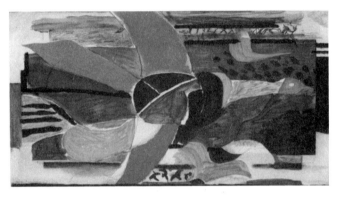

Connoisseurs of Prints by **Sloan.** Etching. 20th century. Lyons Trust.
Oiseau Multicolore by **Braque.** Lithograph. 20th century. Lyons Trust.
Tetlow I by **Feininger.** Etching. 20th century. Lyons Trust.

were just as often populated by a riot of primitive animals and humans.

Pablo Picasso and Georges Braque, still drawing identifiable images, began experimenting with flattened and distorted geometric shapes in a style that came to be known as **Cubism**. **Expressionism** found its voice in the artistic social commentary of the avant-garde German Expressionists **Die Brücke** (The Bridge). A group including Käthe Kollwitz, Emil Nolde, and Max Pechstein produced deeply moving images with woodcuts, while John Sloan and George Luks of the **Ash Can School** worked in etching. At the same time the shift to nonobjective art and pure abstraction began in Germany with the work of Wassily Kandinsky and Franz Marc in a movement called **Der Blaue Reiter** (The Blue Rider). Its influence can be seen later in the work of Paul Klee and Lyonel Feininger. **Futurism**, **Constructivism**, **Dadaism**, and **Surrealism** are among the variants of the work begun by Picasso, Braque, and Matisse in the first decades of the twentieth century and flourished along with the **Bauhaus** in the art deco period.

Nachdenkende de Frau by Kollwitz. Lithograph. 20th century. Lyons Trust.

In addition to their regular paintings and graphics, a group of artists including Paul Klee, Pierre Bonnard, Georges Braque, Pablo Picasso, Henri Matisse, Raoul Dufy, Marc Chagall, Georges Rouault, Ferdinand Léger, Jacques Villon, Joan Miró, and Salvador Dalí were approached by imaginative publishers and contracted to illustrate elaborate books and portfolios. Known as "peintres-graveurs" because they worked in both painting and graphics, many of these young artists were just at the beginning of their careers and soon became known as the **École de Paris**. Artists from all over the world traveled to Paris in these early years of the twentieth century to be part of the vibrant art scene. Like the publishers who were gathering young

Circus Study by **Miró.** Lithograph. 20th century. Lyons Trust.
La Pêche by **Dufy.** Woodcut. 20th century. Lyons Trust.
Girls at Counter by **Bishop.** Etching. 20th century. Lyons Trust.
Sueño by **Rivera.** Lithograph. 20th century. Lyons Trust.

Group Portrait with Dog & Cat by **Sekino.** Woodblock. 20th century. Lyons Trust.
Winter in Aizu by **Saito.** Woodblock. 20th century. Lyons Trust.
Untitled Landscape by **Munakata.** Woodblock. 20th century. Lyons Trust.

artists under their wing, the reappearance of the print workshop brought young emerging artists together under various roofs to practice their craft in a more economical and convivial way. Often a modern print will identify, along with the artist, the publisher or workshop where the image was printed. Imprimerie Lacourière, Atelier Mourlet, Atelier 17, George Miller & Son, Tamarind, and Gemini are some of the most important workshops of the twentieth century.

The twentieth century saw a number of earlier printing processes revisited, refined, and combined. Several variations of the relief process appear at this time. The linocut, originally done on linoleum, now appears on rubber and cardboard matrixes. Embossing used an un-inked relief block pressed onto the dampened paper to produce a raised line within the colored surface. The woodcut saw a renaissance in the wide-ranging imaginations of artists like Paul Gauguin, Raoul Dufy, Pablo Picasso, Marc Chagall, Edvard Munch, Emil Nolde, Käthe Kollwitz, Wassily Kandinsky, Paul Klee, M. C. Escher, Lyonel Feininger, László Moholy-Nagy, Eric Gill, Rockwell Kent, Jose Posada, Leonard Baskin, and Antonio Frasconi, all of whom used this technique at one time or another. Sent to Japan after World War II, a group of American artists (including Jack Perlmutter) revived and retrained a group of young printmakers in the art of the woodblock print. With exposure to contemporary western influences some artists like Junichiro Sekino and Kiyoshi Saito modernized the traditional genres of portraits and landscapes, while others like Shiko Munakata worked in abstractions.

As printing became increasingly mechanized and driven by the need for larger and more economical editions, lithographic stones were replaced first by zinc and then by tin or aluminum plates. The lithographic crayon was replaced by lithographic rubbing ink. Artists like Edvard Munch, Käthe Kollwitz, Henri Matisse, Pablo Picasso, Stow Wengenroth, Grant Wood, Thomas Hart Benton, John Steuart Curry, Ben Shahn, Jackson Pollock, and Frank Stella found lithography to be an art form that complemented their paintings.

Several new stencil processes gained popularity in the Art Deco period. **Pochoir** was a process used extensively in the 1920s by artists like Georges Barbier and Romaine de Tirnoff (Erté). Silk screening developed as another variant of the stencil process. The term serigraph was invented to distinguish fine art prints from commercial silk screen art. Artists like Ben Shahn, Marcel Duchamp, Robert Rauschenberg, Andy Warhol, Robert Indiana, Frank Stella, Sister Mary Corita, Jack Perlmutter, and Roy Lichtenstein worked extensively with serigraphs.

The twentieth century also saw renewed interest in intaglio processes. Engravings, etchings, and mezzotints were used singularly or in combination. The monotype, which had been used experimentally by Paul Gauguin, Edgar Degas, Pablo Picasso, Henri Matisse, and Marc Chagall, came into its own during the twentieth century. Processes were used individually or in combination, depending on the various skills of the artist, the quality of materials available to him, and the techniques he was experimenting with at that particular time.

As the Great Depression spread across Europe and America, art took on a bleaker and more propagandistic tone. There was no money for art supplies and no buyers for those artists who continued to be productive. The support of artists by the American government in the form of the Federal Art Project of the

Supermarket by Shahn. Silkscreen. 20th century. Lyons Trust.

*The Fence
Mender* by
Benton.
Lithograph.
20th century.
Lyons Trust.

Descending
by Bibelk.
Serigraph.
20th century.
Lyons Trust.

WPA (Works Progress Administration) was a major factor in the development of another generation of American artists. The work of William Gropper, Stuart Davis, Ben Shahn, Willem de Kooning, Jackson Pollock, Grant Wood, Rockwell Kent, and Thomas Hart Benton reflected the harsh realities of everyday life in America—life in the city tenements, struggles in the work place, the barrenness of the farm, and the ever-present political struggles of a people seeking to integrate and improve their lives.

After World War II, the contemporary art scene exploded. All kinds of imagery, styles, techniques, and printing processes were now valid—as long as they sold—and anybody could claim to be an artist . . . even a gorilla! (In December 1997, the Terrain Gallery in San Francisco presented a show of acrylic paintings on canvas that received very positive reviews from critics who did not know the identity of the makers. The "artists" were, in fact, two very talented lowland gorillas, Koko and Michael, for whom painting was a favorite creative outlet. Koko and Michael had been trained in sign language, and seemed able to understand and express emotions and to handle abstract concepts.) You can see why it is difficult to assess who will be the most important artists a hundred years from now.

As prices for oil paintings soared, prints became the medium of choice for the beginning collector. Artists who were originally painters became printmakers as they

Monotype:
Shaman by Fay. 20th century. Lyons Trust.

saw the market and their income potential expand. Prints became larger and more lavishly colorful in order to replicate the impact of oil paintings and justify higher prices. Any surface became acceptable as a matrix or medium, and in fact three-dimensional prints combined multiple mediums such as metal, stone, glass, fiberboard, plastics, and resins together to provide a single design surface. Old processes reappeared with new refinements, and combinations of multiple processes became common in designing a print. Editions that had gone from uncounted numbers in the late nineteenth century to meticulously numbered and identified images at the beginning of the twentieth century now appeared as "monotypes," with only a single printing possible. Color, originally done with a series of plates dedicated to a particular color and printed successively, now could be done from a single plate to produce different patterns within an edition. Laborious graphic processes were simplified, and the artist became less involved in the production of the print as he turned more of the process over to his printer.

New artists appeared with new labels, and their prints reached a newer and younger audience. Robert Motherwell, Helen Frankenthaler, Jackson Pollock,

Etchings & Drypoints by **Diebenkorn.** Aquatint and drypoint. 20th century. Lyons Trust.
Campbell's Soup Can on Shopping Bag by **Warhol.** Silkscreen. 20th century.
Lyons Trust.
Sunrise by **Lichtenstein.** Offset lithograph. 20th century. Lyons Trust.

and Franz Kline were proponents of **Abstract Expressionism**, while Frank Stella is identified with **Abstract Illusionism**. **Pop Art**, whose most famous practitioners include Andy Warhol and Roy Lichtenstein, focused on found objects and images that appeared in the mass media. **Op Art** used colors and shapes in motion to create optical illusions. **Minimal Art** used modulated color and oversimplified form to minimize the subject, style, and personality of the artist. Warhol, Wayne Thiebaud, Robert Rauschenberg, Claes Oldenburg, and Lichtenstein were all influenced by these movements. Other major and minor artists found expression in Transavantgardism, **Chicago Imagism,** and **Neurotic Realism.**

The last quarter of the twentieth century saw dramatic changes in the printmaking process. Even the time-honored definition of an "original" print was put into question because of the artist's limited involvement in the process. Automated or photographic composition involves the artist only in the initial stages of conception. The rest of the process is left to skilled photographers, technicians, and printers, which many feel is technology and not art, much less original art. Others contend that these prints are original because the artist creates the design of the print and, therefore, he is not reproducing an already existing work of art. Throughout the 1960s the debate raged on with numerous attempts to define and redefine what exactly constitutes an "original print." Into this controversy came computer graphics, which only further complicated the matter. With these prints, the computer is the medium and the artist writes a program that details the composition. The program feeds into the computer, and the design is drawn onto paper with a stylus or plotter or printed onto paper by any one of several computer-compatible printers. The image is then photographically transferred onto a silk screen and printed.

Another confusing addition to the print field has been the giclée print. While its technology is highly detailed and it is produced under the artist's supervision as a limited edition, it is nonetheless an expensive reproduction as are the limited edition facsimiles of the work of now dead artists.

This chapter has covered a lot of material—perhaps too much to take in all at once—but you will find that the collecting of prints is like working a great jigsaw puzzle. As you look at what pleases you in a particular print, you will also be looking at the kind of process, the style of imagery, and the nature of the period that define the history of that particular print. Attention to these basic elements will help you develop what I like to call the "educated eye." ◼

3
THE ABC'S OF COLLECTING PRINTS

The easy availability of well-designed and well-executed graphics enables art lovers to develop collections that grow out of their special interests while enhancing the spaces in which they live and work. By purchasing fine prints of good quality, it is possible to build a collection that provides a lifetime of aesthetic enjoyment while (we hope) the art steadily increases in value. The complex world of graphics is a highly specialized part of the art market, and buying prints can be a little confusing at first for the beginner. As I'll show below, it can really be quite enjoyable.

WHAT IS AN ORIGINAL PRINT?
To begin with, it is important to understand what an original print is *not*. It is not in any way a reproduction or copy of another work of art. An "original print" is the artist's conception of a unique idea printed

during the artist's lifetime, on paper or a similar material employing one or more of the processes described here. The intention to create an original print is the key to the originality of the finished work. From start to finish, the original print is under the control of the artist. He or she chooses the subject, the technique, and the printing process, and controls the quality of the impression and the number of copies to be printed. If the print is pulled after the artist's death, that print is no longer an *original print* but rather a *restrike*. Restrikes are invariably inferior because they are not printed under the artist's supervision. These graphics should command a far cheaper price in the marketplace but are often intentionally or inadvertently sold as fine original prints.

Secondly, an original print is not one of a kind, but rather one of a series of apparently identical images. Because there is always more than one impression of each print, "original" does not mean "unique." However, while the basic image remains the same, the condition and clarity can be markedly different from impression to impression.

Finally, not everything that has the label of an original print is in reality an actual original print. *Caveat emptor*—buyer beware! Many shops and stalls in the United States and abroad are filled (either knowingly or unknowingly) with reproductive art from master prints to modern graphics. Always be sure that any information a salesperson gives you about your print is written on your sales slip, as the sales slip is your legal contract with the dealer. If you work with reputable dealers, they will gladly provide detailed documentation on your purchases and stand behind their inventory. When you become more familiar with prints, you will be comfortable in identifying different processes, papers, and coloring on your own.

WHAT MAKES A COLLECTOR?

A collector is someone who assembles around himself objects that he enjoys. They can be timeless or trendy, inexpensive or extravagant, flat or multidimensional. The key here is that the focus is on the person who is collecting, not what is being collected.

Art is a very personal experience. A collector is in the business of making choices—some good, some not so fortunate. Often, however, we can learn more from our bad choices than from our good choices.

Getting ready to start a collection involves several steps. Think about what pleases you in art you've looked at in the past: art in magazines, in museums, at shows, or even in hotels. Visit galleries, art and antique shows, garage sales, and surf the Internet. Subscribe to periodicals that focus on styles that you like or those that provide educational information on prints. Begin to put aside money earmarked for art purchases.

When you are ready to actually begin collecting, start with a journal-like notebook and write down your impressions. This will help you focus your interests over a period of time and give you a basis for comparison as you begin your search. When you are ready to actually examine a print, have a checklist. Begin by trying to identify specific things that please you in that particular piece. Ask the owner to let you look at the print in good light and away from the clutter of other objects or prints. If you are looking at the art on a flat surface, always prop it up against a wall as well so that you can see how the image works vertically and horizontally. Determine the style or period of the print. *Always* evaluate the condition. If the print is framed, will they open the frame so you can see any trimming, gluing, repairs, or mat burn? How would you describe the quality of that particular impression? Find out the provenance of the print—where has it been all this time? Write down your impressions and any information you find or are told about the artist or this particular image, and don't forget to note the price. Even if this is not the print for you, writing down all the details will clarify your impressions and give you something to refer to later.

Collecting prints in not a new concept. From the introduction of the printing press, graphic arts were highly collectible. Created to provide a means of communication and education for the widest possible audience (most of whom couldn't read), they conveyed a message that had wide appeal and needed no words to be understood. Unlike today's publications, where an idea can move from concept to press in a matter of months, yesterday's projects could take years to get into print. The earliest graphics were published individually or in small segments and pasted into boxes, bibles, and cabinets to protect and preserve them. Private or ecclesiastical commissions provided part of the money to finance the printing and feed the artist, and consequently, subject matter was often limited by the interests of the donors. The seventeenth century saw prints sought after and collected for their subject matter—often biblical, allegorical, historical, or scientific—and/or for the reputation of the artist. Prints could be single, freestanding illustrations or set into a matrix and surrounded with text. As graphic processes became more technically advanced, a group of master printers emerged with images so skillfully executed and artistic that they are still among the most sought-after prints of all time.

In the eighteenth century and the early part of the nineteenth century, there were two kinds of collectors: the wealthy sponsors who would collect a complete study and keep it as part of their library, and the emerging middle classes who would buy individual images for education or amusement. Prints had to tell a story visually, so details were important. Prints were purchased individually or by subscription so that the same image printed at the same time could have been bound or not bound, depending on who purchased it. Many prints were discarded shortly after viewing, much like our newspapers today; others were saved as the beginning of a collection. The social and industrial revolutions of the mid-nineteenth century forever changed the nature of collecting. The sheer volume of images available, coupled with the Victorian impulse to cover every inch of space with decoration, produced the concept of purely decorative images that could be hung on the wall. Print rooms, where graphics were basically used as wallpaper and hung floor to ceiling, were in vogue, and even the humblest cottages had decorative graphics framed on the walls.

In the centuries before the introduction of air conditioning and central heating, paper was particularly vulnerable to the vicissitudes of dampness, darkness, and various pests. Consequently, preservation and storage were haphazard at best. If a print had continuing interest, it could be preserved by pasting it in a scrapbook, a collection book, or in another book, such as a family bible. Another storage favorite was the book press or some other flat and weighted substitute. Gentlemen would often keep their prints in portfolios and invite young ladies to "come up and see my etchings." In any case, the combination of changing fashion and interest, wear and tear of everyday life, and destruction from war and pestilence made for a short "shelf life" for the average print.

WHERE CAN I PURCHASE ORIGINAL PRINTS?

Museums and libraries are rarely in the business of selling art, although there are times when they deaccession prints in their collections. They are, however in the business of collecting art, and you can often buy informative catalogues from their special featured exhibits. Most museum print collections are not on public view but can be seen by appointment. Curators are not usually available to the public and, while they can provide scholarly information about a piece, they will not offer advice or evaluate the price of a print. So this is a very limited source for actually purchasing original prints.

Art dealers are obviously in business to sell art. They can be found in their brick and mortar galleries, at vetted art and antique shows, and even on the Web. Begin with dealers with whom you feel comfortable. A good dealer is friendly and knowledgeable, allows you to browse in his gallery, and listens and responds to your questions. He will have done "due diligence" and be able to provide information on the artist, title, process, date, condition, and price of each print you are examining. Membership in professional organizations indicates that a dealer has met specific educational and ethical standards. A reputable dealer will offer a detailed bill of sale and will refund the purchase if it turns out to be not as described. Many dealers will exchange a purchase as your needs or tastes change, will allow you take things out on approval, and will help you locate a particular print if they don't have it in stock.

Auction houses often include prints in their general sales, and larger houses will have specialized print sales as well. You can physically preview a sale or rely on the auction catalogue for descriptions and estimated prices. Unlike the Hollywood versions of auctions, you do not automatically become a buyer by inadvertently scratching your head. If you intend to bid you will be asked to register when you arrive. Be sure to read the conditions of sale. You should determine within your own mind the price you are willing to pay before the auction begins so as not to be carried away in the bidding. Remember that there can be mail and phone bids already submitted and that the seller has the right to place a reserve price below which he will not sell. The auctioneer determines the increments of bidding and finalizes the sale. When the sale is over, many auction houses will, for a fee, provide information on prices received for the prints actually sold. The price you will pay will include an additional percentage commission to the auction house as well (a "buyer's premium"). The advantage of buying at auction is the excitement of the event and the opportunity to snatch some overlooked bargain. The disadvantage is that you have no way of ascertaining the true condition of a print when it is already framed, and condition is one of the most important determinants of fair market value.

One of the first graphics my husband and I bought when we first started collecting many years ago was an eighteenth-century etching of the Colosseum in Rome by Piranesi. We had been at an auction and bought it on impulse. If we had been more experienced or had looked at some of his other works, we would have realized that, without being able to see the image unframed, that it was not a lifetime impression but a restrike, nor could we know that it had been trimmed, glued to cardboard, and burned by a non acid-free mat. We were so pleased to have bought a Piranesi for twenty-five dollars that we were blinded to the clues that would have shown us that it was in fact a posthumous impression in poor condition. Today it is still worth only twenty-five dollars. About the same time we also bought, after much study and guidance from a venerable New York dealer, a small, carefully documented Rembrandt second-state lifetime etching for twenty-five dollars. (This was in the 1950s when gas was only twenty-five cents a gallon.) That impression has appreciated well over two thousand percent.

The increasing importance of the Internet in the marketplace deserves to be mentioned. Most major museums and galleries have a Web site where you can view their collections and learn about the artists they specialize in, as well as their business practices. (See the resource guide, page 82.) Other dealers without actual galleries have Web sites that provide much the same information. There are also untold numbers of individuals without any particular expertise or credibility who are selling what may or may not be original prints of varying condition and quality. The key to successful bids and purchases is asking questions before bidding or purchasing any print. Check the evaluations that previous purchasers have given the seller. Here again, the plus side is the fun and efficiency of surfing the Web and comparing what is available from your laptop. The minus side is the difficulty of dealing with a disappointing purchase or a seller who is no longer in business.

Finally, there is the ever-present flea market, street fair, or garage sale to add to the thrill of the hunt. While the occasional treasure can be found for pennies on the dollar, the inability to determine the true condition of a print makes it a pure gamble.

HOW DO I BEGIN COLLECTING?
Rule #1: Buy what you love.

The primary motive for buying a work of art is usually aesthetic, and there are more than five hundred years of graphic imagery from which to choose, encompassing an almost unlimited range of subject matter and style. There is real joy and excitement in looking, finding, and purchasing an original piece of graphic art. Begin by looking for prints that relate to a personal interest or fill a particular decorative need. Don't be afraid to examine and explore styles that are unfamiliar or uncomfortable. Look for dealers who will let you exchange prints in the future if your tastes change or as you upgrade your collection. Whatever you do, collect what you like and not what you think will make a good investment someday in the future. It is by pursuing your genuine interests that you'll naturally become a more discriminating collector, and you will learn almost effortlessly to tell the fine from the ordinary.

Rule #2: Train your eye.

The best way to develop a discriminating eye and choose art that will provide longtime pleasure is to study museum collections, art books, and decorating magazines, and visit reputable dealers in their galleries or at art, antique, and book fairs. Each period in art reflects a particular style or interest. Each artist has his own particular visual signature, and his techniques will either fit the style of the period or rebel against it. Look for the styles that appeal to your particular taste, and the techniques that please you the most. Begin your education with books, magazines, and the Internet. Save or mark images that you are particularly drawn to. Look at how a print fits into the general style of the period and the artist's body of work. While this will get you started, it won't substitute for actually looking at the real thing. Pay particular attention to the details within the print. No page or screen can convey the subtleties of paper texture, color hue, clarity of detail, and overall condition. Visit museums and art galleries. Ask questions. Take advantage of the knowledge, experience, and tastes of the experts. Discuss what makes a particular print special. As you explore the world of graphic art, you will develop an "educated eye."

Rule #3: Always buy the best you can afford.

Just as they say the most important thing to keep in mind when buying real estate is "location, location,

location," the most important thing that determines value with a print is "condition, condition, condition." Inferior prints should be purchased only if they are particularly rare or temporarily fill a hole in a collection and should be replaced as soon as a better quality image can be found. Always buy the best condition you can afford at the time. *Top quality will always bring top price! Poor condition will always be poor condition!*

WHAT SHOULD I COLLECT?

Start with something that grabs your interest. Look at it, learn about it, and look at it again. Don't reject something just because it doesn't appeal to you at first glance. Just as there are many styles of graphics, there are many approaches to collecting prints. One may concentrate on the works of a single artist or group of artists, or a specific period, process, or subject.

Artists: If you decide to collect the works of a particular artist, remember that simply because a print is by your favorite artist, it does not necessarily mean it is valuable. Every artist has good and bad days. An artist's early work usually commands slightly less because he hasn't matured, and his later work may be tired and repetitive. In addition, late in life he may be producing a large quantity of work to ensure his income flow, making the value less than his earlier limited editions. The benefit of concentrating on the work of a single artist is that you can see the vitality and evolution of his art. As he matures he will undoubtedly experiment with different colors, shapes, and techniques, so your collection will never be boring.

Periods: If you choose to focus your collection on a particular period or school, remember that art is a field of evolving fashion. (We are talking here about changes in taste among buyers and collectors; the evolution of styles among artists themselves, though related, is quite a different matter.) Something that is popular now may not be in vogue a few years from now. The elaborate engravings of the rococo period were popular in the 1920s; today they are out of style. The black and white engravings of the Art Deco and

Depression periods were abandoned when prosperity returned and are only now regaining popularity. Impressionist printmakers have been favorites for over a hundred years. Who knows how time will evaluate what is popular today?

Processes: I have not encountered many people who collect prints of only one kind of process, but I can see how collecting a particular kind of process could be appealing if it had a kind of cohesive unity to its look. Chiaroscuro woodcuts, Japanese woodblocks, and drypoint etchings come to mind as possibilities.

Genres: You may find that particular subjects hold the most appeal for you. There are so many genres that you're bound to find one you really enjoy. Botanicals, architecture, and maps have great visual appeal and have long been popular. Perhaps you will find that you prefer landscapes or animals, or even non-representational subjects.

Many collectors feel, however, that the most satisfying approach is to search for prints that relate to personal interest or fill a particular decorative need. Remember that collections evolve and tastes change, so take your time as you begin.

WHAT DETERMINES VALUE?

Why is it that what appears to be two of the same print can command different prices in different places? Prices vary for a number of reasons. One dealer can have paid more for a print than another, one may have many galleries to support while the other works from home, one may have put hours into "due diligence" before selling the print, and another may simply be turning it around quickly for a profit.

Value is based on equivalent prices in comparable markets. Pricing is always subjective. In the end, the value boils down to what a given buyer is willing to pay a given seller on any particular day. While processes are relatively easy to identify, there are no hard and fast rules, no one thing that allows an expert to determine the value of a print. Experts use a group of criteria, plus their experience, to find an appropriate value.

Authenticity: It is impossible to judge the authenticity of a print without seeing it in person. An expert looks at the paper, the inks, and the references in the catalogue raisonné that identify the state and edition, and then compares the print to other prints from the same edition to determine authenticity. He or she will also pay attention to the provenance of the print if available—who sold it, who bought it, and in what collections and exhibitions it may have been included. (See also the following section, "How Do I Know If a Print Is Real?")

Reputation of the artist: Is the artist established and well known? Is he an emerging artist or is he past his prime? What is the significance of this particular print in the lifetime work of that artist? Is the artist known for his prints or is he better known in other mediums? For example, Winslow Homer got his start illustrating the Civil War with wood engravings for *Harper's Weekly*. After the war he began doing wood engravings of the scenes of everyday American life that later became the trademark of his oil and watercolor paintings. This gives these earlier prints their uniquely desirable position in the marketplace.

Size of the edition: How many images of this print were produced originally? How many different states or editions did the artist pull in his lifetime? Generally, earlier states are more valuable than later states. Are the plates still in existence? Are they being reissued?

Quality of the impression: Is there anything unique about this particular image? Is there a mistake that could increase or decrease the value and did the artist subsequently make corrections in later editions? Is the impression crisp and clean and the registration of the color accurate? Is there a residue of ink along the plate mark indicating a very early pull?

Condition: Condition is probably the most important criterion in valuing a print, and different sellers will use different terms in describing their graphics. Ideally the best condition is that which finds a print as close to its original condition as when first printed or published. Prints that meet this criterion are often termed in "excellent" or "mint" condition. Prints that are otherwise in fine condition are often termed "very good" or "good." These are the prints normally found in galleries and exhibitions and are the ones you should seek out. Prints termed "fair" are those that have suffered wear and tear and that you are most likely to find in the general marketplace. Prints that are identified as "poor" have substantial defects, damage, or distress.

Some defects are easily identified—others are harder to spot. *Trimmed* indicates that the paper size is not as originally printed and that the print does not retain its full margins. *Acidification* or acid burn indicates that the previous matting or framing has actually burned the paper and turned it brown. Left uncorrected, the paper will eventually be destroyed. *Foxing* is a fungus growth that produces brown or green spots on the paper and occurs when a print is stored in a dark or damp place. It can be stabilized or removed by a professional restorer, but if left unattended it will continue to spread across the image. Insect and pest damage can result in worm holes, fly spots, or chewed edges. *Wear* can indicate several conditions: thin or rubbed surfaces, water stains, notations in pen, pin holes, creases, or folds. Prints that have been glued down to cardboard, dry-mounted, or hinged and mounted with masking or transparent tape need to be noted as such.

Added or recent color is another negative in valuing prints. The most desirable coloring is identified as "original" or "contemporary" color, meaning it was done at the time or in the period that the print was issued. Coloring not of the same period destroys the intrinsic value of the print, leaving only whatever decorative value one finds in it. Your eye will help you decide whether the color in an antique print is original or not. Period coloring was done with vegetable dyes made from the grasses, berries, and herbs found locally, except for blue which had to come from the indigo plant. These vegetable colors are muted and beautifully shaded and always completely translucent. You should be able to see every line of the design through the color. Aniline dyes were introduced in the mid-nineteenth century and are brighter and more opaque. They operate with a very different palette of colors, such as yellow-greens, turquoise, and orange. A word of caution: There is a whole industry of people working by the light of their television sets coloring old black-and-white prints with modern dyes. When buying colored prints always be sure your sales slip indicates not only the date of the print but also *the date the coloring was done!*

Scarcity in the marketplace: Another determinant of value is the scarcity of a particular image in the marketplace—how hard it is to find for sale at any given point of time. Several things enter into the rarity of a print:

1. How many images were produced originally and how many are still around?

2. Is there anything unique or historically significant about this particular image?

3. How popular is the subject matter? Like clothing, art goes in and out of style. Early in the history of prints, religious scenes were popular. Today there is only a limited market for them. In the eighteenth and nineteenth centuries, beautiful landscapes and genre scenes were in vogue. By the twentieth century, tenements and factories were in favor. Roses and tulips will always be more popular than dandelions, elaborately dressed lords and ladies than peasants and waifs, warmer colors than cooler colors. As this book goes to press, palm tree prints are so popular that you would have a hard time finding one anywhere!

4. Size and shape can also be important. Larger prints were expensive and limited in number even at the time they were printed. Given the vicissitudes of time and the destruction caused by innumerable wars, not to mention the problems of storing and caring for large pieces, it is understandable that they will always be more expensive than smaller prints produced at the same time. In the same way, since the majority of prints published were vertical images, horizontal images are harder to find and are there-

fore more expensive. Interestingly, round and oval prints are hard to sell.

You can see that value depends on many criteria, but in the end, it boils down to supply and demand in the marketplace. The noted Chicago auctioneer Leslie Hindeman relates a good example that summarizes what we've been discussing. A man bought a framed print for a few dollars at a flea market simply because he liked the frame. When he took it apart he discovered a printed copy of the Declaration of Independence dated July 4, 1776. He thought it was a fake but decided to have it appraised, only to discover that in fact it was real. It was sold at auction in 1991 (in what was then a roaring economy) for $2.4 million. That buyer tried to sell it in 1993 (during a recession in the economy), but there were no buyers. It was offered again in 2000 (before the dot-com bubble burst) and sold for $7.4 million. Clearly something besides inflation and the ups and downs of the economic cycle must have factored into this dramatic price rise. Research along the way found that this print was one of only thirty-five copies known to be remaining and that all of the others were either in museums or promised to museums. This print was the only one that could conceivably become available and/or remain in private hands, making it priceless.

Determining the market value of prints is the job of a qualified appraiser. As appraisers, we are able to evaluate the variables described above and assign a dollar amount based on the price of a comparable print in similar condition in recent worldwide markets. When choosing an appraiser, check professional qualifications and affiliations (not all certified appraisers are equipped to deal with the specifics of graphic art). An appraiser should have no vested interest in the print (it is unethical to buy a print that you are appraising) and should charge a flat fee rather than a percentage of the amount valued. There are two different kinds of appraisals. The first looks at *current market price* to determine replacement or donation value. The second, which is commonly used in estate or divorce settlements, values the print at its *wholesale cost*.

HOW DO I KNOW IF
A PRINT IS REAL?

From the beginning of the printing process, fakes, forgeries, restrikes, and reproductions abounded! Copper plates were passed from generation to generation within a family, from one firm to another—printed and reprinted, corrected and reprinted yet again. In the fifteenth and sixteenth centuries, knowledge was so limited and information moved so slowly that it was not uncommon to reprint earlier images in later editions long after the artist was gone. Original sixteenth- and seventeenth-century plates that were still in existence were collected, reworked, and reprinted. Cartographers added new discoveries to old maps, while new publishers acquired the plates of many of the great artists, such as Rembrandt and Dürer, and reworked and reissued them. The demand for more detailed and informative images in the seventeenth and eighteenth centuries paralleled the explosion of knowledge and the restructuring of society that was occurring.

So, how do you know if you are looking at an original print or a restrike done hundreds of years later? The first thing that an expert looks at is the paper on which a graphic is printed. Handmade paper has identifying characteristics due to the particular processes used to make that sheet in a certain time period. Fifteenth-, sixteenth-, and seventeenth-century papers were "pressed." The fibers are somewhat raised and "nappy" to the touch. Eighteenth-century papers are shaken on a screen and when held up to the light show horizontal and vertical lines as well as the mark of the maker. Nineteenth- and twentieth-century paper is rolled through a press, producing an even and smooth surface. Many twentieth-century fine art prints have returned to handmade and watermarked papers that are identified in the catalogue raisonné, or list of works, for each artist.

Working with high-power magnification, an expert next examines the inks that are used in printing the image. Fifteenth- and sixteenth-century inks are made of either animal, vegetable, or mineral (squid, charcoal, ground semiprecious stones), and under magnification will form what looks like a hollow trough: darker black on the outside edges and lighter black in the center. Seventeenth- and eighteenth-century inks are usually India ink and under magnification string out, showing filaments. Inks after the Industrial Revolution are aniline chemical inks and under magnification, a residual grain-like sand can be seen.

Finally, the expert checks the reference books to be sure that the image is correct. Is the print the same size as the original when published? Is the medium used the same as in the original publication? Has it been copied from another image? Interestingly, in many reproductions (whether produced mechanically or by hand), the print will be a mirror image of the original, with the right and left sides reversed.

Art work that has been copied photographically is not an original print but rather a reproduction. Early photographic and offset images can by fairly easily identified by working with a high-powered magnifying glass (I like the double- or triple-loupe magnifiers that are sold in photography stores). Look for colors and lines that break down into uniform and repetitive patterns: dots, dashes, octagons, and hexagons. Modern offset and digital printing, however, has become so sophisticated and computer color analysis so accurate that magnification is not much help and the expert must again return to evaluating the paper and inks.

HOW DO I TAKE CARE OF MY PRINTS?

Although antique prints have been around for centuries, their care has been haphazard at best. The Industrial Revolution was truly a revolution, not only of mechanical process but in ways of thinking as well. In a society in which a product can become obsolete overnight and disposability has become the norm, it is not surprising that until recently we failed to note what was happening to fine paper. Today paper suffers not so much from the ravages of time as from the effects of nineteenth-century products and pollutants.

A collector should make a habit of practicing good conservation procedures as part of the collecting process. While there are no legal standards for conservation, the Library of Congress has set some criteria for storing and matting paper as a benchmark for preserving works of art on paper. The Professional Picture Framers Association and the FACTS Organization (Fine Art Care and Treatment Standards) have published conservation guidelines for the framing industry. The American Institute for Conservation has pioneered research and education in conservation and restoration practices.

Speaking of restoration, be aware that the purpose of restoration is to repair damage already done. As with dentistry, restoration is not a do-it-yourself project, but rather a highly skilled technical field. A professionally trained restorer will look at the print itself and give you a detailed report on the condition and causes of the deterioration and an analysis of the methods and choices needed to repair the situation, along with a time and cost estimate. No matter how skillfully done, restoration does change the value of a print and may in fact change the quality of the image itself. It can remove the sizing and raise the paper surface so that the image appears fuzzy. It can cause the colors to fade or bleed or it may cause the paper to disintegrate and be lost entirely. Remember, it is always worthwhile to put the effort into conservation—it may save you from having to deal with a print's restoration.

To see this more clearly we must understand how fragile paper actually is. We need to exercise great care when handling a print. Always be sure that your hands are clean. Even so, you may want to use cotton gloves to prevent the fatty acids on your skin from transferring to the paper surface. Hold the print on both sides, between your thumbs and forefingers. Never turn or pick up a print by the corners—the weight and strain on the paper could easily make it tear or crease.

Remember that paper "breathes" and that temperature and humidity control are extremely important. Fluctuations in temperature and humidity cause paper to expand and contract, giving off or absorbing water vapor that can lead to buckling, microbiological infection, dust, a host of paper destroying insects, and manmade pollution. (Did you know that dust has sharp edges that can actually scratch the surface of a print as it settles?)

While most of us have filtered light conditions in the areas where we are displaying our art, too much or too little light can cause real problems. Exposure to strong light can cause fading and disintegration. Too little light can allow fungus growth to get a foothold and spread. When storing prints, always be sure that your art is in contact with only acid-free materials. Unframed materials should be stored flat between sheets of rag paper in acid-free boxes or portfolios. Most dealers keep their prints in specially designed containers known as Solander boxes. These sturdy boxes are lined with acid-free paper, and their hinged lid allows you to slide prints from one side to the other without having to turn them over.

HOW SHOULD I FRAME MY PRINTS?

Today most of us choose to display our print collections rather than store them. When hanging your prints, particular thought should be given to conservation. Proper procedure calls for a mat and mounting board of one-hundred-percent cotton rag. The print is attached to the mounting board behind the mat with acid-free hinges and framed with some kind of ultraviolet filtering glass or acrylic. If your print was framed several years ago, it would be wise to have it checked and perhaps redone to these standards.

While conservation is the primary concern in framing, most of us have aesthetic concerns as well. Frames and mats are expensive, and choosing them can be a confusing and overwhelming task. Next to choosing the print itself, choosing a framer is possibly the most important decision that will affect your long-term investment in art. Just as there are many kinds of print dealers, there are many kinds of framers. You can do it yourself quickly and inexpensively by buying ready-made mats (yes, even acid-free mats) and frames in an art or photography store. Many art supply stores will have framing departments where you can try different mats and frame corners and get some help in assembling a frame order. Custom framers, however, will have had professional training and most likely have several years of apprenticeship. They will be knowledgeable and current about the materials they are using and aware of what is new in color and design. They will explain the materials they are suggesting and offer several appropriate design options. Think about framing as you would about buying a sofa. You can walk in and purchase one from the floor, or order one where you have some choice of fabric. You can work with a designer and have one customized with different arm and back styles, or, depending on how much you're prepared to spend, you can have a sofa entirely custom-built to your exact specifications.

Keep in mind that there are many appropriate framing solutions for any piece of art. Think about how you want a print to work in your home or office and remember that the function of a mat and frame is to separate the art from other colors and shapes in a room. If you want your print to be a focal point in the room, you will want to use a gold- or silver-toned frame because these colors reflect light and will draw your eye to the print immediately. If you want your print to blend into the totality of the room, you will probably choose a wood or black frame. If you have several prints in your collection and limited wall space, there are quick-change framing systems available so that, if the prints are matted uniformly, you can rotate the images yourself at will.

There are two kinds of frame choices currently available. *Stick* or *length moldings* are made of prefinished hardwood, metal, or plastic that has been cut to size, joined with mitered corners, and secured with brads or nails. If the molding is gold or silver the color is an inexpensive metal leaf and often the burl wood effect is photographic rather than part of the wood itself. Closed corner frames are made from unfinished wood that has been hand-carved, hand-stained, and/or hand-gilded with twenty-two karat gold or silver leaf. The corners are joined with spines and covered in several applications of glue, gesso, and clay to build up surface so that the mitered corners are concealed.

While you have a wide range of choices in designing the matting for your print, remember that the aesthetic purpose of the mat is to focus your eye on the print itself. The simplest mat is a plain rag presentation mat. You can add depth by using different thicknesses of mat board (like eight- or twelve-ply instead of the usual four-ply) or by adding detail with gold or colored lines. A double rag mat uses contrasting color mats, one overlaying the other, leaving a quarter inch of the underlying color exposed. Another popular mat is the classic French mat. French mats were introduced in the eighteenth century when artists began to do engraved borders around their prints. A traditional French mat will have a panel surrounding the print of a custom-mixed watercolor with additional color or gold lines. Variations can include marble papers, ribbons and/or elaborate corner designs, hand-drawn flowers, leaves, or bows. Or you can use no mat at all by suspending ("floating") the image on a backboard so that the edges are visible.

Glazing is another important factor in framing, as it protects the print from dust, fingerprints, and sunlight. When choosing between glass and acrylic, glass is generally less expensive; however, it sometimes has a color shift toward green that mostly goes unnoticed. Where the color shift of glass is distracting (because of its iron content), acrylic is a better choice. Choose acrylic also for larger prints or for pieces that might be at risk of breaking during shipping or in an earthquake, as the material is light and will not shatter. Acrylic does require special attention to avoid scratching or damage incurred from incorrect cleaning (no products with ammonia can be used). Regular glass or acrylic filters out forty percent of the sun's ultraviolet ("UV") rays. Conservation or UV glass or acrylic filters out ninety-five percent of the ultraviolet rays. Non-glare, the glazing we all love to hate, may sometimes flatten, cloud, and distort the image. Newer antireflective glass and acrylic is the preferred choice by collectors, galleries, and museums where controlled lighting conditions exist.

A word about hanging pictures, an art unto itself. Avoid hanging prints too high (you can't see them) or too low (they blend into the furniture). Many people like the irregularity that a group of odd-numbered prints provides, but there is nothing wrong with hanging prints in pairs or even-numbered groupings. In fact, there are no rules at all—you can do whatever pleases you! When my husband and I were first married, our collection grew to be larger than our wall space and we had no storage, so we hung pictures from the ceiling to the floor. We were asked to let our little cottage be included in a tour to raise money for a local charity, and as the guests poured through the house, I overheard a group of ladies ask their decorator, "Is it all right to hang pictures from floor to ceiling?" The decorator's response was, "Honey, if you've got them, you can hang them any way you want." ◼

4

THE INSTANT EXPERT QUIZ

1. What makes any print an original?

2. What is a restrike?

3. What is a reproduction?

4. What is a woodcut?

5. What is an engraving?

6. What is an etching?

7. What is a lithograph?

8. What is a silk screen/serigraph?

9. What is a state?

10. What is a catalogue raisonné?

11. What does signing and numbering signify?

12. What is a proof?

13. What determines value?

14. What does an appraiser do?

15. What is original color?

16. What is conservation matting and framing?

17. What kind of prints should I buy?

18. What information should be on your sales slip, and why is it important?

19. What is an "instant expert" in graphic art?

Answers

1. An artist's conception of a unique idea printed on paper or similar material by one or more processes in his lifetime.

2. A posthumous printing of a graphic.

3. A copy or facsimile of another work of art.

4. A raised design carved from a block of wood.

5. A design cut into a metal plate.

6. A design cut into a coated metal plate with a special tool.

7. A design drawn on a stone or plate with a crayon-like substance.

8. A design pressed through an opening in a screen or mesh.

9. Each time an artist chooses to print images from a plate.

10. A reference book that details an artist's work.

11. The artist authenticates and identifies a particular print.

12. A trial pull of a print before publication.

13. Reputation of artist, size of edition, quality of a print, as well as condition and rarity in the marketplace.

14. Provides a current evaluation of value based on equivalencies in marketplace.

15. Color applied at the time or in the period of the original printing.

16. Acid-free and ultra-violet filtering materials used in presentation.

17. Buy what you love and buy the best you can afford at the time.

18. Your sales slip is your legal contract and should contain the title of the print, the name of the artist, the country of origin, the date of printing, and anything that affects condition and the price.

19. An "instant expert" is somebody who uses both knowledge and experience to develop an "educated eye." ◼

RESOURCE GUIDE

I. MUSEUMS AND COLLECTIONS

There are few, if any, museums, libraries, and collections devoted exclusively to the graphic arts, but all of them do have print rooms where their collections can be viewed by appointment, as well as libraries where you can research prints, and special print exhibits periodically (usually with an accompanying catalogue). In addition, they house the paintings of some of the greatest graphic artists of all time, and it is really interesting to compare their work in mediums other than the print.

Wherever possible, instead of addresses, phone numbers, and business hours, I've given Web sites because they usually provide the most current and accurate information.

UNITED STATES

California: Los Angeles Area
Getty Museum (www.getty.edu/museum)
Huntington Library (www.huntington.org)
Los Angeles County Museum (www.lacma.org)
Museum of Contemporary Art (www.artcommotion.com)
Norton Simon Museum (www.nortonsimon.org)

California: San Francisco Area
Asian Art Museum (www.asianart.com)
Cantor Center (http://ccva.stanford.edu)
de Young Museum (www.thinker.org/deyoung)
Legion of Honor (www.thinker.org/legion)
Museum of Modern Art (www.sfmoma.org)
Oakland Museum (www.museumca.org)

Connecticut
Wadsworth Atheneum (www.wadsworthatheneum.org)
Yale University Art Gallery (www.yale.edu/artgallery)

District of Columbia
Freer Gallery (www.asia.si.edu)
Library of Congress (www.loc.gov)
National Gallery (www.nga.gov)
Phillips Collection (www.phillipscollection.org)
Smithsonian Institute (www.si.edu)

Illinois
Art Institute of Chicago (www.artic.edu)

Indiana
Indianapolis Museum (www.ima-art.org)

Maryland
Baltimore Museum of Art (www.artbma.org)
Walters Art Gallery (www.thewalters.org)

Massachusetts
Boston Museum of Fine Arts (www.mfa.org)
Fogg Museum (www.artmuseums.harvard.edu)
Isabella Stewart Gardner Museum
(www.gardnermuseum.org)

Michigan
Detroit Institute of Arts (www.dia.org)

Minnesota
Minneapolis Institute of Arts (www.artsmia.org)
Walker Art Center (www.walkerart.org)

Missouri
Nelson Atkins Museum (www.nelson-atkins.org)
St. Louis Art Museum (www.slam.org)

New York
American Museum of Natural History (www.amnh.org)
Brooklyn Botanical Garden Library (www.bbg.org/lib)
Cloisters (www.metmuseum.org)
Cooper-Hewitt (www.cooperhewitt.org)
Dahesh Museum of Art (www.daheshmuseum.org)
Frick Collection (www.frick.org)
Guggenheim Museum (www.guggenheim.org)
Metropolitan Museum of Art (www.metmuseum.org)
Morgan Library (www.morganlibrary.org)
Museum of Modern Art (www.moma.org)
New-York Historical Society (www.nyhistory.org)
New York Public Library (www.catnyp.nypl.org)
Whitney Museum (www.whitney.org)

North Carolina
North Carolina Museum of Art (www.ncartmuseum.org)

Ohio
Cleveland Museum of Art (www.clemusart.com)
Toledo Art Museum (www.toledomuseum.org)

Oklahoma
Thomas Gilcrease Museum (www.gilcrease.org)

Pennsylvania
Barnes Foundation (www.barnesfoundation.org)
Hunt Botanical Library (http://huntbot.andrew.cmu.edu)

Institute of Contemporary Art (www.icaphila.org)
Philadelphia Museum of Art (www.philamuseum.org)
Andy Warhol Museum (www.warhol.org)

Texas
Amon Carter Museum (www.cartermuseum.org)
Dallas Museum of Art (www.dm-art.org)
Kimbell Art Museum (www.kimbellart.org)

CANADA

Musée National de Beaux-arts de Quebec
(www.mmfa.qc.ca/en/index.html)

EUROPE

Austria
Kunsthistorisches Museum (www.khm.at)

France
Bibliothèque Nationale (www.bnf.fr)
Centre Georges Pompidou (www.cnac-gp.fr)
Louvre (www.louvre.fr/louvrea.htm)
Musée d'Orsay (www.musee-orsay.fr)

Germany
Alte Pinakothek (www.pinakothek.de)

Ireland
Trinity College Library (www.tcd.ie/Library)

Italy
Galleria dell'Accademia
(www.polomuseale.firenze.it/accademia)
Arengario Museo del Novecento (to open in 2007)
Borghese Gallery (www.galleriaborghese.it)
Palazzo Pitti (www.palazzopitti.it)
Uffizi Gallery (www.polomuseale.firenze.it/english/uffizi)
Vatican Museum
(http://mv.vatican.va/3_EN/pages/MV_Home.html)

Holland
Mauritshuis Museum (www.mauritshuis.nl)
Rijksmuseum (www.rijksmuseum.nl)
Van Gogh Museum (www.vangoghmuseum.nl)

Russia
Hermitage (www.hermitage.ru)

Spain
Guggenheim Bilbao (www.guggenheim-bilbao.es/ingles/
home.htm)
Museo d' Art Contemporani de Barcelona
(www.macba.es)

Museo del Prado (http://museoprado.mcu.es)
Reina Sofia Museum (http://museoreinasofia.es)

Switzerland
Kunstmuseum (www.kunstmuseumbasel.ch)

United Kingdom
British Library (www.bl.uk)
British Museum (www.british-museum.ac.uk)
Courtlauld Institute Gallery (www.courtauld.ac.uk)
National Gallery (www.nationalgallery.org.uk)
Tate Gallery (www.tate.org.uk)
Tate Modern (www.tate.org.uk/modern)
Victoria and Albert Museum (www.vam.ac.uk)
Wallace Collection (www.the-wallace-collection.org.uk)

ASIA

Japan
Mori Art Museum
(www.mori.art.museum/html/eng/index.html)

AUSTRALIA
Art Gallery of New South Wales
(www.artgallery.nsw.gov.au)
Museum of Contemporary Art (www.mca.com.au)
National Gallery of Victoria (www.ngv.vic.gov.au)

II. OTHER RESEARCH RESOURCES

ONLINE REFERENCE RESOURCES
Art History Research Centre (www.harmsen.net/ahrc)
The Burlington Magazine (www.burlington.org.uk)
House & Garden Television (www.hgtv.com)
Library of Congress, Prints & Photographs On-Line
Catalogue (www.loc.gov/rr/print/catalog.html)
Mother of All Art History Sites
(http://art-design.umich.edu/mother)
Union List of Artist's Names Browser (ULAN) Getty
Vocabulary (www.getty.edu/research/conducting_research/
vocabularies/ulan)
Program (www.getty.edu/research/tools/vocabulary/
ulan/index.html)

ART PERIODICALS
Apollo (www.apollo-magazine.com)
Art & Antiques (www.artandantiques.net)
Art & Auction (www.artandauction.com)
Art News Magazine (www.artnews.com)

Art Newspaper (www.theartnewspaper.com)
Journal of the Print World
(www.journaloftheprintworld.com)
Print Quarterly (www.printquarterly.com)

PERIODICALS WITH OCCASIONAL ARTICLES ON PRINTS

Antiques Magazine (www.themagazineantiques.com)
Architectural Digest (www.archdigest.com)
Arts & Antiques Weekly (www.thebee.com)
Catalogue of Antiques & Fine Arts
(www.antiquesfinearts.com)
Country Living (www.hearstmags.com)
Elle Decor (www.elledecor.com)
House Beautiful (www.hearstmags.com)
House & Garden (www.houseandgarden.com)
Smithsonian Magazine (www.smithsonianmagazine.com)
Southern Living (www.southernliving.com)
Traditional Home (www.traditionalhomes.com)
Veranda (www.veranda.com)

PRICE GUIDES

Art Fact (www.artfact.com)
Gordon's Print Annual (www.gordonsart.com)

STOLEN ART IDENTIFICATION

Art Loss Register (www.artloss.com)
Department of Culture, Media & Sport (DCMS, United Kingdom) (www.culture.gov.uk)

III. PROFESSIONAL ASSOCIATIONS

ART & PRINT ASSOCIATIONS

American Antiquarian Society
(www.americanantiquarian.org)
American Historical Print Collectors Society
(www.ahpcs.org)
Art Dealers Association of America (ADAA)
(www.artdealers.org)
Associated American Artists (www.artresources.com)
Fine Art Dealers Association (FADA) (www.fada.com)
International Fine Print Dealers Association (IFPDA)
(www.printdealers.com)
International Map Collectors' Society (IMCoS)
(www.imcos.org)
Print Council of America (www.printcouncil.org)

ANTIQUE ASSOCIATIONS

Antiques Council (www.antiquescouncil.com)
Art & Antique Dealers League of America
(www.artantiquedealersleague.com)
British Antique Dealers Association (BADA)
(www.bada.org)
Confederation Internationale des Negociants en Oeuvres
d'Art (www.cinoa.org)
Association of Art & Antique Dealers (LAPADA)
(www.lapada.co.uk)
National Art & Antiques Dealers Association (NAADAA)
(www.naadaa.org)

APPRAISAL ASSOCIATIONS

American Society of Appraisers (ASA)
(www.appraisers.org)
International Society of Appraisers (ISA)
(www.isa-appraisers.org)

CONSERVATION ASSOCIATIONS

American Institute for Conservation of Historic and
Artistic Works (AIC) (http://aic.stanford.edu)

IV. PLACES TO BUY PRINTS & SUPPLIES

DEALERS SELLING PRINTS

Aaron Galleries. Chicago, IL
(www.artline.com/galleries/aaron/aaron.html)
Alexandre Antique Prints Maps & Books. Toronto,
Canada (www.alexandremaps.com)
Alice Adam Ltd. Chicago, IL (www.aliceadam.com)
Advanced Graphics. London, UK
(www.advancedgraphics.co.uk)
Agnew's Gallery. London, UK (www.agnewsgallery.com)
Brooke Alexander Editions. New York, NY
(www.baeditions.com)
Allison Gallery, Inc. Storrs, CT
(www.allisonstorrsgallery.com)
Annex Galleries. Santa Rosa, CA
(www.annexgalleries.com)
W. Graham Arader Galleries. Houston, New York,
Philadelphia, San Francisco (www.aradergalleries.com)
Arion Press. San Francisco, CA (www.arionpress.com)
Richard B. Arkway, Inc. New York, NY (www.arkway.com)
Richard Reed Armstrong Fine Art. Chicago, IL
(www.armstrongfineart.com)
Ars Libri Ltd. Boston, MA (www.arslibri.com)

The Art of Japan. Bellevue, WA (www.theartofjapan.com)

Frederick Baker, Inc. Chicago, IL
(www.frederickbakerinc.com)

Anne & Jacques Baruch Collection Ltd. Chicago, IL
(information at annebaruch@aol.com)

Belgis-Freidel Gallery Ltd. Syonset, NY
(www.toulouselautrecposters.com)

Valeria Bella Stampe. Milan, Italy (www.valeriabella.com)

James A. Bergquist. Newton Centre, MA (Box 246.
Newton Centre, MA 02459-0246)

Joel R. Bergquist Fine Arts. Stanford, CA (information at
prints@northrup-jones.com)

Berkeley Square Gallery. London, UK (www.bsgart.com)

Bethesda Art Gallery. Glen Echo, MD
(www.printdealers.com/member_template.cfm?id=15)

Michele Birnbaum Fine Art. New York, NY (information at
mbfany@nyc.it.com)

Galerie Simon Blais. Montreal, Canada
(www.galeriesimonblais.com)

C. G. Boerner, Inc. New York, NY (www.cgboerner.com)

Devin Borden Hiram Butler Gallery. Houston, TX
(www.artdealers.org/members/borden.html)

Boss Fine Art. Boston, MA (www.bossbooks.com)

Robert Brown Gallery. Washington, DC
(www.robertbrowngallery.com)

Gary Bruder. New York, NY (information at
gblautrec@aol.com)

Catherine E. Burns Fine Prints. Oakland, CA
(www.catherineburns.com)

Burton Marinkovich Fine Art. Washington, DC
(www.burtonmarinkovich.com)

William P. Carl Fine Prints. Northampton, MA
(www.williampcarlfineprints.com)

Eric G. Carlson Fine Prints & Drawings. New York, NY
(information at e.carlson@worldnet.att.net)

Cartographic Arts. Peterswburg, VA
(www.cartographicarts.com)

Jo Ann & Richard Casten Ltd. Old Field, NY
(www.castenmaps.com)

William McWillie Chambers III. New York, NY
(information at mcwilliechambers@earthlink.net)

Chicago Center for the Print. Chicago, IL
(www.prints-posters.com)

Childs Gallery. Boston, MA (www.childsgallery.com)

Taylor Clark Gallery. Baton Rouge, LA
(www.taylorclark.com)

Sylvan Cole Gallery. New York, NY (101 West 57th St.
New York, NY 10019)

Conner-Rosenkranz. New York, NY (www.crsculpture.com)

Alan Cristea Gallery. London UK (www.alancristea.com)
Crown Point Press. San Francisco, CA
(www.crownpoint.com)
Merlin C. Dailey & Associates. Victor, NY
(www.merlindailey.com)
Elizabeth Danechild Japanese Prints. San Francisco, CA
(information at danechild@inreach.com)
Davidson Galleries. Seattle, WA
(www.davidsongalleries.com)
Jeanne Davidson Fine Prints. New York, NY
(information at jdavi@excite.com)
Dolan/Maxwell. Philadelphia, PA
(www.dolanmaxwell.com; information at
dolmax@mindspring.com)
Dranoff Fine Arts. New York, NY (www.dranofffineart.com)
Durham Press Inc. Durham, PA (www.durhampress.com)
Edition Schellmann Inc. New York, NY
(www.editionschellmann.com)
Egenolf Gallery. Burbank, CA (www.egenolfgallery.com)
G.W. Einstein Company Inc. New York, NY (information at
GWECO@aol.com)
Equinox Gallery. Vancouver, BC (www.equinoxgallery.com)
The Fine Art Society. London, UK (www.faslondon.com)
Fitch-Febvrel Gallery. New York, NY
(www.fitch-febvrel.com)
Flowers Graphics. London, UK (www.flowerseast.com)
Madeleine Fortunoff Fine Prints. Locust Valley, NY
(information at msfort@optonline.net)
Leonard Fox Ltd. New York, NY (www.foxrarebooks.com)
Douglas Frazer Ltd. Medina, WA (www.theartofjapan.com)
Thomas French Fine Art. Fairlawn, OH (Box 13410,
Fairlawn, OH 44334)
Francis Frost. Newport, RI (www.frostprints.com)
Abigail Furey Fine Prints. Brighton, MA
(www.fineprintcollecting.com)
Galerie André Candillier. Paris, France
(www.candillier.com)
Galerie Grillon. Paris, France (information at
galeriegrillon@noos.fr; galeriegrillon@cybercable.fr)
Galerie Lareuse. Washington, DC
(www.originalprints.com; information at
GalerieLareuseDC@aol.com; jml@ct.ezvousart.com)
Galerie Laurencin. Lyons, France (www.laurencin.net)
Galerie Lelong. New York, NY (www.galerie-lelong.com)
Galerie R.G. Michel. Paris, France (17 Quai Saint-Michel,
Paris, France F-75005)
Galerie St. Etienne. New York, NY (www.gseart.com)
Galerie Seydoux Estampes et Dessins. Paris, France
(information at galerie.seydoux@magic.fr)

Galleri K. Oslo, Norway (www.gallerik.com)

Galleria Grafica Tokio. Tokyo, Japan
(www.gallery.to/grafica)

Gallery 539. New Orleans, LA (539 Bienville, New Orleans,
LA 70130)

Gallery Saint-Guillaume. Tokyo, Japan (information at
saint104@ma.kcom.ne.jp)

Galeria Toni Tapies. Barcelona, Spain
(www.tonitapies.com)

Pia Gallo. New York, NY
(information at piaart@aol.com)

Garton & Co. Devizes, UK (www.gartonandco.com)

Gemini G.E.I @ Joni Moisant Weyl. New York, NY
(www.joniweyl.com)

Roger Genser—The Prints & the Pauper. Santa Monica,
CA (Box 5133, Santa Monica, CA 90409-5133)

Israel Goldman. London, UK (information at
izzygoldman@btconnect.com)

C. & J. Goodfriend Drawings & Prints. New York, NY
(www.drawingsandprints.com)

Gordon's Art. Phoenix, AZ (www.gordonsart.com)

Goya-Girl Press & Contemporary Art Gallery. Baltimore,
MD (www.goyagirl.com)

Conrad R. Graeber Fine Art. Riderwood, MD
(www.conradgraeber.com)

Graphicstudio University of South Florida. Tampa, FL
(www.graphicstudio.usf.edu)

William Greenbaum Fine Prints. Gloucester, MD
(www.greenbaumprints.com)

Bobbie Greenfield Gallery. Santa Monica, CA
(http://artscenecal.com/BGreenfield.html)

Harco Gallery. Wilson, WY (www.harcogallery.com)

Pegram Harrison Fine Art, Inc. Bloomington, IN
(www.pegramharrison.com)

Jane Haslem Gallery. Washington, DC
(www.janehaslemgallery.com)

Donald Heald Books Maps & Prints. New York, NY
(www.donaldheald.com)

Leen Helmink Antique Maps. Netherlands
(www.helmink.com)

Hill-Stone, Inc. New York, NY (Box 273, Gracie Station,
New York, NY 10028)

Hirschl & Adler Galleries, Inc. New York, NY
(www.hirschlandadler.com)

Catherine Hodgkinson. London, UK
(www.hodgkinsonart.com)

Dorianne Hutton Fine Art. Greenwich, CT (information at
dhuttonfineart@aol.com)

Susan Inglett Gallery & I. C. Editions. New York, NY

Jan Johnson Old Master & Modern Prints. Montreal, Canada (information at janjohn@total.net)

R. S. Johnson Fine Art. Chicago, IL (www.rsjohnsonfineart.com)

Jane Kahan Gallery. New York, NY (www.janekahan.com)

E. H. Ariens Kappers. Amsterdam, Netherlands (www.masterprints.nl)

Jim Kempner Fine Art. New York, NY (www.artnet.com/jkfa.html)

Kennedy Galleries. New York, NY (www.kgny.com)

Keichel Fine Art. Lincoln, NE (www.kiechelart.com)

E. & R. Kistner Kunstantiquariat. Nuremberg, Germany (www.kistner.de)

Barbara Krakow Gallery. Boston, MA (www.barbarakrakowgallery.com)

Ernest S. Kramer Fine Art. Wellesley, MA (www.kramerfineart.com)

Kraushaar Galleries. New York, NY (www.artnet.com/gallery/626/Kraushaar_Galleries_Inc.htm)

Greg Kucera Gallery. Seattle, WA (www.gregkucera.com)

Landfall Press, Inc. Chicago, IL (www.landfallpress.com)

August Laube Kunstantiquariat. Zurich, Switzerland (information at augustlaube@augustlaube.ch)

Josef Lebovic Gallery. Sydney, Australia (www.joseflebovicgallery.com)

Barbara Leibowits Graphics Ltd. New York, NY (www.barbaraleibowitsgraphics.com)

R. E. Lewis & Daughter. San Rafael, CA (www.relewis.com)

R. M. Light & Co. Santa Barbara, CA (information at rmlight@silcom.com)

Ann Long Fine Art. New York, NY (www.annlongfineart.com)

Kay Lopata. Wycombe, PA (www.kaylopatafineart.com)

Lyons Ltd. Antique Prints. Palo Alto, CA (www.LyonsLtd.com)

Jorg Maass Kunsthandel. Berlin, Germany (www.deutscherexpressionismus.de)

Ian Mackenzie Fine Art. London, UK (information at ian.mackenzie@dial.pipex.com)

Malbert Fine Arts. Chicago, IL (521 Dickens Ave., Chicago, IL 60614; 773-348-3543)

The Map House of London. London, UK (www.themaphouse.com)

Mathew Marks Gallery. New York, NY (www.matthewmarks.com)

Marlborough Graphics. London, UK (www.marlboroughfineart.com)

Marlborough Graphics. New York, NY
(www.marlboroughgallery.com)

Marsha Mateyka Gallery. Washington, DC
(www.marshamateykagallery.com)

Martinez A. & D. Estampes Anciennes & Modernes.
Paris, France (www.martinez-estampes.com)

Paul McCarron Fine Prints. New York, NY
(www.paulmccarron.com)

Jerald Melberg Gallery. Charlotte, NC
(www.jeraldmelberg.com)

Galerie Marion Meyer. Paris, France (information at
galeriemarionmeyer@hotmail.com)

Tobey C. Moss Gallery. Los Angeles, CA
(www.tobeycmossgallery.com)

Frederick Mulder. London, UK (information at
info@frederickmulder.com)

Jonathan Novak Contemporary Art. Los Angeles, CA
(www.novakart.com)

O'Hara Gallery. New York, NY (information at
info@oharagallery.com)

Old Print Shop. New York, NY (www.oldprintshop.com)

Joel Oppenheim. Chicago, IL (www.audubonart.com)

Pace Prints. New York, NY (www.paceprints.com)

Paramour Fine Arts. Franklin, MI
(www.paramourfinearts.com)

Paulson Press. Berkeley, CA (www.paulsonpress.com)

Pettibone Fine Art. New York, NY
(www.pettibonefineart.com)

Philadelphia Print Shop. Chestnut Hill, PA
(www.philaprintshop.com)

Pillsbury Fine Prints. Paris, France (104, rue du Bac, Paris,
France 75007; information at pfprints@aol.com)

Marilyn Pink Master Prints & Drawings. Los Angeles, CA
(www.marilynpink.com)

Platt Fine Art. Chicago, IL (www.plattfineart.com)

Poster Treasures. Paris, France (38, rue Boileau, Paris,
France 75016; information at posters@noos.fr)

Jonathan Potter Maps. London, UK (www.jpmaps.co.uk)

Pratt Contemporary Art. Sevenoaks, Kent, UK
(www.prattcontemporaryart.co.uk)

Proofs Ltd. London, UK (www.proofs-ltd.co.uk)

Paule Proute. Paris, France (information at
Proutesa@wanadoo.fr)

Remba Gallery-Mixografia Workshop. West Hollywood,
CA (www.rembagallery.com)

Purdy Hicks Gallery. Bankside, London, UK
(www.purdyhicks.com)

Redfern Gallery Ltd. London, UK (www.redfern-
gallery.com)

Lutz Riester. Freiburg, Germany (Wollflinstrasse 9, Freiburg, Germany D-79104; 011-49-761-352-15)

Marc Rosen Fine Art Ltd. New York, NY (www.marcrosenfineart.com)

Helmut H. Rumbler Kunsthandel. Frankfurt, Germany (Gothestrasse 2, D60613 Frankfurt, Germany; 011-49-69-291-142)

Howard Russeck Fine Art. Gladwyne, PA (www.russeckgallery.com; 1125 Woodmont Road, Gladwyne, PA 19035; 610-519-9141)

Mary Ryan Gallery. New York, NY (www.maryryangallery.com)

Leslie Sacks Fine Art. Los Angeles, CA (www.lesliesacks.com)

William H. Schab Master Prints. New York, NY (information at whsmasterprints@aol.com)

Rona Schneider. Brooklyn Heights, NY (www.ronaschneiderprints.com)

Scolar Fine Art/Gordon Samuel. London, UK (www.scolarfineart.com)

Segura Publishing Company. Mesa, AZ (www.segura.com)

Shark's Ink. Lyons, CO (www.sharksink.com)

William Shearburn Gallery. St. Louis, MO (www.artnet.com/wshearburn.html)

Susan Sheehan Gallery. New York, NY (www.susansheehangallery.com)

Sims Reed Ltd. London, UK (www.simsreed.com)

Smith Andersen Editions. Palo Alto, CA (www.smithandersen.com)

Solo Impression, Inc. New York, NY (www.soloimpression.com)

Henry Sotheran Books. London, UK (www.sotherans.co.uk)

Sragow Gallery. New York, NY (www.sragowgallery.com)

Carolyn Staley-Fine Japanese Prints. Seattle, WA (www.carolynstaleyprints.com)

Stanza del Borgo Srl. Milan, Italy (information at silvatagl@tin.it)

Andrew Stasik Fine Arts. Darien, CT (www.astasikfinearts.com)

Stewart & Stewart. Bloomfield Hills, MI (www.stewartstewart.com)

Sarah Stocking Fine Vintage Prints. San Francisco, CA (www.sarahstocking.com)

M. Lee Stone Fine Prints. San Jose, CA (www.mleestonefineprints.com)

Stone & Press Gallery. New Orleans, LA (www.stoneandpress.com)

Paulus Swaen. Indian Rocks Beach, FL (www.swaen.com)

Tamarind Institute. Albuquerque, NM (www.unm.edu/~tamarind/gallery.html)

Tandem Press. Madison, WI
(www.tandempress.wisc.edu/tandem)
Egon and Joan Teichert Fine Prints. Hauppauge, NY
(www.eteichertfineprints.com)
Susan Teller Gallery. New York, NY (information at
stg568@aol.com)
The Tolman Collection. New York, NY, and Tokyo, Japan
(www.tolmantokyo.com)
Tooley, Adams & Co. Oxfordshire, UK (www.tooleys.co.uk)
Ursus Books & Prints Ltd. New York, NY
(www.ursusbooks.com)
Guy van Hoorebeke. Bruges, Belgium (Boomgaardstraat
7, Bruges, Belgium 8000; 011-32-50-333-507)
Van Straaten Gallery. Steamboat Springs, CO
(www.riverhouseeditions.com)
Verne Collection, Inc. Cleveland, OH
(www.vernegallery.com)
Diane Villani Editions. New York, NY
(www.villanieditions.com)
Mark J. Weinbaum Fine Vintage Posters. New York, NY
(information at mjweinbaum@aol.com)
William Weston Gallery. London, UK
(www.williamweston.co.uk)
Weyhe Gallery. Mt. Desert, ME (information at
libris@prexar.com)
Winter Works on Paper. New York, NY
(www.winterworksonpaper.com)
Wolfgang Wittrock Kunsthandel. Berlin, Germany
(www.wittrock-art.de)
Works on Paper Inc. Philadelphia, PA
(www.worksonpaper.biz)
Worthington Art. Chicago, IL (information at
worthingtonart@aol.com)
Gerhard Wurzer Gallery. Houston, TX
(www.wurzergallery.com)
Charles M. Young Fine Prints. Portland, CT (information
at cy@cmyoungfineart.com)
Zaplin Lampert Gallery. Santa Fe, NM
(www.zaplinlampert.com)

V. SHOWS SELLING PRINTS

GUIDE BOOKS TO SHOWS
Arts & Antiques Weekly (The Bee) Annual Guide to
American Antique Shows (www.thebee.com)
Art Newspaper Annual Guide to International Art Fairs &
Antique Shows: The Year Ahead
(www.theartnewspaper.com/tya.html)

Catalogue of Antiques & Fine Arts Red Book Semi-annual Guide to Fairs (www.antiquesfineart.co.uk)
International Guide to Art Fairs and Antique Shows (www.artandantiquesfairguide.com)
Town & Country Semi Annual Guide (www.hearst.com/magazines)

ART SHOWS

ADAA Art Show—New York (www.artdealers.org)
Affordable Art Fair—New York (www.affordableartfair.com)
Art Basel (www.artbasel.com)
Art Basel Miami (www.artbasel.com)
Art Chicago (www.artchicago.com)
Art Cologne (www.artcologne.de)
Art Frankfurt (www.Artfrankfurt.de)
Art Toronto (www.tiafair.com)
IFPDA Print Fair (www.printfair.com)
London Original Fine Print Fair (www.londonprintfair.com)
Los Angeles Art Show (www.fada.com)
New York IFPDA (www.printfair.com)
Works of Art on Paper—New York (www.sanfordsmith.com/wop.html)

ANTIQUE & ART SHOWS

Biennale des Antiquaires—Paris (www.biennaledesantiquaires.com)
Chicago Antiques Fair (www.merchandisemart.com/chicagoantiques)
Connoisseur's Antiques Fair (www.artantiquedealersleague.com)
Cultura: Art & Antiques Fair-Basel (www.culturabasel.com)
Grosvenor House Art & Antiques Fair (www.grosvenor-antiquesfair.co.uk)
International Asian Art Fair—New York (www.haughton.com)
International Fine Arts Fair—New York (www.haughton.com)
Kunst-Messe München (Munich) (www.kunstmessemuenchen.de)
Los Angeles Antique Show (www.losangelesantiqueshow.com)
Milano International Fine Art & Antiques Show (Milan) (www.milano-antiques-show.com)
MilanoInternazionale Antiquariato (Milan) (www.expocts.it/mia)
New York Antiquarian Book Fair (www.sanfordsmith.com/nyabookfair/index.html)

Olympia Fine Art & Antique Fairs (www.olympia-antiques.co.uk)
Original Miami Beach Antique Show (www.dmgworldmedia.com)
Palm Beach Classic Art & Antique Fair (www.dmgworldmedia.com)
Pavilion des Antiquaires–Paris: *See Biennale des Antiquaires*
San Francisco Fall Antiques Show (www.sffas.org)
TEFAF Maastrich (www.tefaf.com)
Venice Biennial (www.labiennale.org)
Winter Antique Show (www.winterantiquesshow.com)

MODERNISM ART SHOWS
ARCO Modern & Contemporary Art Show—Madrid, Spain (www.arcospain.org)
Art Forum Berlin (www.art-forum-berlin.com)
Art of the Twentieth Century—New York (www.sanfordsmith.com/a20.html)
The Art Show—New York (www.artdealers.org/artshow/index.html)
Chicago Modernism (www.dolphinfairs.com)
FIAC—Paris (www.fiacparis.com)
Frieze Art Fair—London (www.friezeartfair.com)
Los Angeles Modernism (http://lamodernism.com)
Melbourne Art Fair (www.artfair.com.au)
Modernism—New York (www.sanfordsmith.com/mod.html)
Palm Beach Contemporary (www.dmgworldmedia.com)
Scope Art Show—The Hamptons, NY (www.scope-art.com)
SOFA—New York (Sculpture, Objects & Functional Art) (www.sofaexpo.com)
SOFA—Chicago (Sculpture, Objects & Functional Art) (www.sofaexpo.com)

SHOW MANAGERS
Casky Lees (www.caskeylees.com)
Daily Mail Group (www.dmgworldmedia.com)
Dolphin Productions (www.dolphinfairs.com)
Marilyn Gould/MCG Antiques Promotions (10 Chicken St., Wilton, CT; 203-762-3525)
Brian Haughton (www.haughton.com)
Keeling Wainwright (Box 333, Cabin John, MD 20818; information at info@blackfineartshow.com)
Susie McMillian Charity Antique Show Management (information at susiemcm@aol.com)
Sanford Smith (www.sanfordsmith.com)
Stella Management (www.stellashows.com)

WEB SITES SELLING PRINTS

Artnet (www.artnet.com)
Catalogue of Antiques & Fine Arts
(www.antiquesandfineart.com)

AUCTION HOUSES SELLING PRINTS

Artcurial (www.artcurial.com)
Bloomsbury Book Auction
(http://Bloomsbury-book-auct.com)
Bonhams (www.bonhams.com)
Bonhams and Butterfields (www.Butterfields.com)
Bonhams and Goodmans
(www.soldbyauctioneers.com.au)
Christie's (www.christies.com)
Dorotheum (www.dorotheum.com)
Doyle New York (www.doylenewyork.com)
Eldred's Auction Gallery (www.eldreds.com)
FinArte Semenzato (www.finarte-semenzato.com)
Freeman's Auction (www.freemansauction.com)
Leslie Hindman Auctioneers (www.lesliehindman.com)
Ketterer Kunst (www.kettererkunst.com)
Kunsthaus Lempertz (www.lempertz.com)
Northeast Auctions (www.northeastauctions.com)
Pacific Book Auction (www.pbagalleries.com)
Phillips de Pury (www.phillipsdepury.com)
Skinner Auction (www.skinnerinc.com)
Sloans and Kenyon (www.sloansandkenyon.com)
Sotheby's (www.sothebys.com)
Swann Auction Galleries (www.swanngalleries.com)
Tajan (www.tajan.com)
Uppsala Auktionskammare (www.uppsalaauktion.se)
Weschler's Auctions (www.weschlers.com)
West Coast Estates Auctiona
(www.internationalauctioneers.com)
Online Auctions (www.online-auctions-i.com)

CONSERVATION SUPPLIES

Brodart (www.brodart.com)
Demco (www.demco.com)
Gaylord (www.gaylord.com)
Hollinger Corporation (www.hollingercorp.com)
Light Impressions (www.lightimpressionsdirect.com)
University Products, Inc. (www.universityproducts.com)

GLOSSARY

À la Poupée
Poupée in French refers to cotton daubs (called dollies in English). A print is *à la poupée* when colored ink has been applied directly to the surface of the plate and worked into the appropriate area of the design using these cotton daubs.

Abstract Expressionism
An American (particularly New York) non-objective movement begun in the 1940s that used dripping lines, broad slashes, and abstract forms to explore contemporary artistic perspectives and emotions.

Acidification
The browning of a print that occurs when it comes into contact with low grade cardboard or paper for an extended period. Over time, the acid in the inferior paper literally burns the print.

After
Refers to a work done in the style of a named artist but executed at a later date.

Algraphy
A lithographic process that uses an aluminum plate rather than a stone.

Antique Print
Any original print published prior to 1900 is considered antique. This cutoff date is not firmly fixed, however, and in many instances original prints made between the year 1900 and World War II are considered to be antique as well.

Aquatint
A process of printmaking in which a design is cut into a metal plate treated with a fine layer of rosin. The plate is then heated and submersed in an acid bath. As the acid bites the plate between the grains of rosin, it creates a rich texture, with the darkness determined by the length of exposure to the acid.

Art Deco
A movement in architecture and furnishing popular in the 1920s and 1930s that incorporated geometric forms and sharp corners in reaction to the delicate curves of art nouveau.

Art Nouveau
A decorative style that originated in France (literally "new art") during the 1890s and lasted until roughly World War I. Characterized by flowing lines, elegant curves, asymmetry, and flower and leaf motifs.

Arts & Crafts
An artistic movement that arose in the late nineteenth century and rebelled against the mass-produced furnishings of the Victorian era by producing simple, handmade pieces that emphasized craftsmanship over ornamentation.

Ash Can School
A group of New York artists who, during the early twentieth century, began to create art that depicted the streets and tenements of the city in a highly realistic and unglamorous fashion.

Attributed to
Believed to be the work of the named artist.

Authenticity
The verification of a print's originality, the attribution of the artist, the details of its history, and the accuracy of its description and condition.

Autographic
Signifies that part or all of the print is done by hand.

Avant-Garde
French for "vanguard." Used to describe artists who challenge accepted ideas by experimenting with new techniques and concepts.

Barbizon School
A group of painters working in or near Barbizon, a town to the southeast of Paris, during the 1840s and 1850s. The group primarily did landscapes, emphasizing a return to nature and the simpler life.

Baren
A small pouch-shaped tool made from braided bamboo that is used to apply pressure to the paper in the making of woodblock prints.

Baroque
A period of design in Europe during the seventeenth and eighteenth centuries, characterized by exaggerated shapes, contrasting light and shadow, dramatic subjects, and a sense of grandeur.

Bauhaus
A movement begun in Germany in the 1920s that sought to use the principles of Cubism in all aspects of the decorative and fine arts.

Bid
An offer to purchase at an auction. It can be made in person, by a designated representative, by phone, or by mail.

Bite
The term used for cutting an etched or engraved line by immersing the plate in acid.

Blind Stamp
An embossed seal impressed onto a print as the distinguishing mark of the artist, the publisher, an institution, or a collector.

Block
A matrix (surface) for relief printing. The most common is a wood block, used primarily for woodcuts or wood engravings, but mediums such as potatoes, rubber, and linoleum can also be used as blocks.

Blueprint
The process whereby chemically treated paper is exposed to an image, submerged in a specially mixed solution, and coated with a stabilizing fixative to create a photographic print.

Book Plate
An image set into a matrix with accompanying text.

Brayer
A roller used in applying ink to plates.

Broadside
A graphic used for large-scale prints, usually advertisements. These are often lithographic but can also be done with woodblock.

Burin
An engraving tool with a burr or rough point at the end used to produce textured lines in drypoint etching.

Burr
The rough edge that is left on either side of the trough when a needle is used to cut directly into an etching plate.

Buyer's Premium
An additional charge assessed to winning bids at auction, typically a fixed percentage of the purchase price.

Canceled
The act of gouging lines or holes across a printing plate in order to render it unusable. This should be done after an edition is complete in order to prevent unauthorized use of the plate in the future.

Carbograph (Carborundum or Carbon Print)
Prints made from a surface covered with carborundum and then mixed with glue, producing a grainy, textured surface much like a mezzotint.

Catalogue Raisonné
A scholarly document that lists individual artists and all their works known at the time of compilation. It includes all essential documentary information as well as critical and/or academic opinions.

Celluloid Print
An intaglio print in which the image is scratched into a sheet of celluloid.

Chiaroscuro Woodcut
A woodcut printed with several color blocks to imitate drawings done in black ink on colored paper.

Chine Appliqué (Chine Collé)
A print in which the image is impressed onto a thin sheet of China paper that has been glued to a stronger, thicker sheet and printed simultaneously.

Chromolithograph
A lithograph drawn on a metal plate and cut mechanically. Color is applied by using a series of stone or metal plates with different portions of the image inked in various colors.

Cliché Verre
A technique of printmaking in which a design is scratched with a needle onto a glass plate that has been covered with black paint. When exposed to light, the glass plate prints like a negative onto photosensitive paper.

Collage
An assemblage of found materials arranged into a composition.

Collector's Mark
A design or monogram chosen by a collector or museum to identify the pieces in their collection. It is usually printed on the back, but sometimes on the face, and often devalues the price of a print. Regardless, the collector's mark is extremely important in establishing provenance, authenticity and, in some cases, quality.

Collograph
A print representing a combination of the relief and intaglio processes. It is printed from a variety of textured materials that have been glued to the plate like a collage.

Collotype
A hybrid of the letterpress and lithography processes. The glass plate is coated with a gelatin base and textured with an inconsistent dot pattern that, when printed, appears as a uniform tone.

Composite Print
A print made from any assortment of techniques used together.

Computer Graphics
In printmaking, this refers to any program written by an artist in computer language and then printed onto paper using a stylus and plotter. This then becomes the matrix for a silk screen and is printed photomechanically.

Conservation
Steps taken to preserve the condition of a print in storage or on display.

Constructivism
A Russian offshoot of Cubism during the 1920s that created art with utilitarian aims and a detached mechanical perspective.

Contemporary
Belonging to the same period of time (but this does not necessarily imply the current time).

Continuous-Tone
A positive or negative photographic image that produces a complete gradation of tone.

Copyright
The legal right of an artist to control the use of his intellectual and creative property.

Crayon Engraving
An eighteenth century process that used an assortment of engraving needles and roulettes to replicate the look of a drawing.

Criblé
A method of texturing the background of a plate by using punches and awls that produce a random spotted look.

Cross-Hatching
A process in engraving that involves drawing a diagonal grid pattern of fine lines to produce shading and add depth.

Cubism
An artistic movement in the beginning of the twentieth century that stressed abstract forms over more

representational elements. The style takes three-dimensional figures and breaks them into flat, over-lapping planes that present the object from various angles simultaneously.

Cyanotype
The reverse of the blueprint process, producing a blue image on a white background.

Dadaism
A movement in art that reacted against bourgeois society and World War I by rejecting all principles of rationality, organization, and aesthetics. The group was given its name in 1916 at Hugo Ball's Cabaret Voltaire in Zurich, when they inserted a knife into a dictionary and randomly selected the word "dada."

Dauber
A stuffed ball or pad used to apply ink to a plate.

Decalcomania
A process wherein ink is applied to one side of a sheet of paper and then the paper is folded in half, printing an exact replica on the opposite side.

Delineavit or Del.
Latin phrase meaning "has drawn it"; most commonly used in identifying the artist of a lithograph.

Diazo Lithography
A form of lithography that uses film to expose an image onto a photo-sensitized plate. Produces a continuous color rather than the dots of a halftone technique.

Die Brücke
A German movement (literally "the bridge") that began in 1905. The group attempted to link the art of the past with the disjointed forms and jarring colors of modern movements.

Digital Graphics
See *computer graphics*.

Dot-Matrix Printing
A technique of printing images by using a pattern of small pinhead dots.

Double Mat
Two mats laid on top of one another, one with a slightly smaller opening so that a thin line of color is exposed next to the image.

Drypoint
A technique of printmaking in which the image is cut into the etching plate with a needle (rather than acid), throwing sharp ridges of metal up on either side of the line. This burr holds extra ink, creating a warm, rich line. Because burr wears quickly, its presence usually indicates an early impression.

Eau Forte
A French term for engraving.

École de Paris (School of Paris)
A general name for the loosely defined group of artists working in Paris in the early twentieth century. Because these artists were drawn from all over Europe, they shared no distinct style, but all showed a leaning toward Expressionism, and their experimentation had a great impact on the nature of artistic forms.

Edition
An edition of a print includes all the impressions published at the same time or as part of the same publishing event. A *first edition* print is one issued with the first published group of impressions (although these are sometimes pre-dated by a proof edition). An *edition de tete* is a special edition of some kind, either limited or deluxe. Also, it should be noted that editions of a print are different from states of a print. There can be several states of a print from the same edition, and there can be several editions of a print all with the same state.

Electron Print
A print done with a special ink made from radioactive material (carbon or sulfur). When sensitized paper is placed in direct contact with the ink, the image is copied exactly and then developed photographically.

Embossed Print
A print made from a plate that, when impressed, creates three-dimensional areas above or below the surface of the paper. When used without ink, it is termed "blind embossing."

Engraving
A type of printmaking in which the design is executed with an engraving needle or burin that cuts thin V-shaped furrows into a metal plate. The ink is then forced into these grooves with a roller and pressed onto dampened paper.

Épreuve d'Artiste (Artist's Proof)
One of the first pulls of a print, used to determine if corrections are needed before publication.

Estampes Originales
A term indicating original prints.

Estate Impression
A later impression (restrike) of an artist's work printed by a family member after his or her death.

Estimate
An approximation of the value of a print, typically based upon recent sales prices.

Etching
A type of printmaking in which the design is cut into a metal plate that has been coated with an acid-resistant material (called a ground). When immersed in an acid bath, the exposed lines are eaten away or "etched," causing depressions that hold ink for printing.

Excudit or Exc.
A Latin word meaning "has published it."

Expressionism
A primarily German movement in the early twentieth century that aimed to reflect the subjective state of the artist's mind rather than the objective external world.

Facsimile
An exact reproduction, done to the same scale and appearance as the original print.

Fair Condition
A term indicating that a print shows somewhat more than normal wear and tear.

Fauvism
The name "Fauves" (literally "wild beasts") was given to an early twentieth century group of French painters. The style was characterized by bright and garish colors that were used arbitrarily to blend together landscape, human figures, and animal forms.

Fax Printing
An original image printed or copied by a facsimile machine.

Fecit or Fec.
A Latin word meaning "has made it."

Fine Art & Historical Prints
The difference between fine art prints and historical or decorative prints is not clear-cut, nor is it understood by all experts in the same way. A fine art print is one where the artist is primarily concerned with the manner of presentation rather than the content, whereas the maker of an historical or decorative print is focused more on the content of the image than its presentation.

Floating
Suspending a print in a too-large frame so that all edges of the paper are visible.

Flocked Print
An image printed with adhesive ink and then dusted with wool fibers to add texture.

Folio
When an oversize sheet of paper is folded in half, it produces a book known as a "folio." The term can also refer to the individual paper size (each sheet measures approximately 12" x 19").

Foxing
The damage that results when bacteria destroys the cellulose content of paper, typically appearing as brown spots that continue to spread unless removed and stabilized.

Framing
Surrounding a print with an attractive structure that protects and supports the paper so that it can be exhibited.

French Matting
A type of mat done with a watercolor wash surrounding the image. Often detailed with additional lines in color or gold.

Frottage
A print made by rubbing ink onto a thin paper that rests on a raised surface.

Futurism
An Italian movement during World War I closely related to cubism; it stressed the movement, speed, and violence of the machine age.

Gauffrage
An engraving process that produces three-dimensional impressions (raised or sunken designs) without adding color.

Giclée
A computer-generated reproduction that is printed on an Iris printer with water-based ink. Can be done on many different kinds of surfaces.

Good Condition
A print that exhibits no major flaws other than normal wear.

Gouge
A chisel with a curved cutting edge for working in wood.

Graphics
A term used in the art world for original prints.

Grattoir (Mace Head)
An engraving tool used to produce texture on a metal plate.

Gravure
A method of printing that uses photo-mechanical processes.

Ground
A non-porous coating applied to a metal plate before etching.

Gum Arabic
A fixative substance made from the sap of acacia trees, used to hold or highlight color in printmaking.

Halftone
A grid screen that has been cut photo-mechanically and produces color gradations by using a pattern of fine dots.

Hand-Coloring
Watercolor, tempera, crayon, or colored pencil applied to a print by hand at the time of publication under the direction of the artist.

Hatching
Parallel or crossed lines of varying thickness and density that produce shaded areas.

Heliogravure
An intaglio process (based on the aquatint) that produces graded tones photo-mechanically.

Hinge
The manner in which a print is attached to a mat.

Image
An artist's design executed in a particular medium.

Impression
A single piece of paper with an image printed on it from a matrix.

Impressionism
A style of painting that developed in France in the late nineteenth century. The Impressionists attempted to capture the general impression of an object or scene by using primary colors and small brushstrokes to simulate actual reflected light.

Impressit or Imp.
A Latin word meaning "has printed it."

Incisit or Inc.
A Latin term meaning "has engraved it."

Incunabula
A general term referring to examples of early printing.

Ink-Jet Printing
Computer printing that uses miniature nozzles to lay ink onto the paper.

Inlaid Plate
A plate set into a larger plate.

Intaglio
A method of printmaking in which the design is first cut into the surface of a plate. These recessed lines hold the ink, and it is then transferred onto paper under pressure. The lines when printed are raised above the surface of the paper while the edges of the plate itself leave an indentation known as a plate mark.

Invenit or Inv.
A Latin term meaning "has designed it."

Iris Prints
Large computer-generated images printed by an Iris ink jet that sprays a fine mist of water-based color to achieve a continuous tone.

Kallitype
A photomechanical process that uses silver nitrate and ferrous salts that, when exposed to light, create a print in brown tones.

Key Block
The block that carries the full design and is used to print the outline of an image. In color printing, all other blocks are made from this master block.

Laid Down
A print pasted to a backing after printing.

Laser Printing
An electromagnetic process wherein a negatively charged drum prints an image onto positively charged paper, allowing for extremely fine resolution.

Lettering

The lettering of a print usually appears below the image and consists of such information as the title, artist, publisher, engraver, and other data.

Letterpress

A relief process in which the image is printed from raised letters or blocks.

Limited Edition

While antique prints were limited in number due to realities such as market demand or the nature of the medium, impressions of modern prints are often limited intentionally in order to create scarcity in the marketplace and thus increase value. These modern limited editions show the individual print number and the total edition number, separated by a slash mark.

Linocut

A relief process done in linoleum in which the background is cut away so that only the line areas of the design are raised to print.

Lithograph or Lith

A printmaking process in which a grease-based drawing is applied to a stone or aluminum plate and then treated chemically. When the surface is kept wet and rolled with ink, the ink will adhere only to the greasy line. The matrix is then run through a high-pressure press, which transfers the image to a sheet of paper.

Mannerism

A style that began in Italy during the sixteenth century, characterized by an elegantly detailed style and the distortion and elongation of the human form.

Margin

The blank area of paper surrounding the body of a graphic image. If untouched, margins are described as "full." If altered, they are identified as "trimmed" or "trimmed to the plate."

Master

The first or original pull of the impression.

Mat
A way of supporting and displaying a print by using a backing board and a front board with a window through which the image is visible.

Mat Burn
The discoloration or browning that occurs in areas that have been covered by a mat that is not acid-free.

Matrix
The surface upon which a design has been drawn, which is then used to make an impression on paper, thus creating a print. Possible matrices include (wood) blocks, (metal) plates, or (lithographic) stones.

Medium
The material and technique employed by an artist for a specific work, through which the matrix is created.

Metalcut
The earliest relief process in which the image was printed from a raised design with its surface textured by randomly punched dots.

Mezzotint
An intaglio process in which the plate is textured with a fine tooth tool known as a mezzotint rocker. When inked, this surface prints a rich, velvety black. The image is then created by smoothing (burnishing) areas to produce lighter tones. Mezzotints are unusual, therefore, in that they create a white image from a black background.

Mildew
A fungus that thrives in dampness and darkness, producing spots of various colors that must be removed and stabilized.

Millimeter (mm)
The unit of measurement used most commonly in assessing prints. To convert millimeters into inches, multiply by 25.4.

Minimalism
A predominantly American school of art that developed during the 1960s. The group rejected expressive content and created works that were non-representational and often machine made.

Mint
An impression whose condition is as close to the original printing as possible. Can also be identified as a "brilliant" or "crisp."

Mixed Media (Multimedia)
A print whose design is created on a single matrix using a variety of printmaking techniques, for example: line engraving, stipple, and etching.

Monotype
An image is drawn or painted onto an unworked plate (can be metal, glass, or Plexiglas) and pressed onto paper to create a single unique print. A second impression can sometimes be pulled from the plate, producing a "ghost" image.

Mordant
The acid solution into which an etching plate is submerged.

Moulette (Drum Wheel)
A tool used to produce texture on a metal plate.

Nature Print
A type of printing that was experimented with during Victorian times. A leaf is impressed into a soft lead plate in such a way that the plant literally engraves itself. When the plate is printed, it produces an exact replica of the original.

Neo-Classicism
A movement that originated in the mid-eighteenth century and attempted to revive the forms and styles of the classical period in ancient Greece and Rome.

Non-Objective
A term used to describe art that is not representational, a subset of abstract art containing no recognizable figures or objects.

Numbered Print
A modern print that has been numbered by hand to indicate it is part of a limited edition. The numbering takes the form of x/y, where y is the total number of impressions in this edition and x represents the spe-

cific number of the print. Antique prints did not need numbers because the edition size was always small.

Octavo
When a sheet of paper is folded into eight equal parts, it produces a book known as an "octavo." The term can also refer to the individual paper size (each sheet measures approximately 6" x 9").

Offset
A print method that uses an intermediary roller to transfer the image from the original medium (i.e., plate) onto paper.

Op Art
Short for Optical Art. A movement in the 1960s in which artists experimented with black and white forms, grid patterns, and sharp color contrasts to create optical illusions.

Original Print
An original print is one designed and produced under the direction of the artist and which meets his specifications as to quality and size of the edition.

Paper
A thin mass of fibers that have been meshed together into a smooth sheet.

Paper is composed of the woody parts of plants such as bamboo, hemp, flax, cotton, mulberry, rice, and silk, from which all impurities have been removed. Handmade papers are shaken so that the fibers intermesh randomly. Laid paper is pressed by hand into a mold, where the wires used to support the paper pulp emboss their pattern into the paper, often creating a watermark. Wove paper is made by machine on a belt and so lacks these laid lines. China paper is a very thin paper, originally made in China, which is used for *chine appliqué* prints.

pH
A measure of the acidity or alkalinity of a substance based on the concentration of hydrogen ions.

Photograph

A mechanically produced image that has been printed from a negative and suspended in an emulsion on the surface of the paper.

Photogravure (Photo Engraving)

A photomechanical process in which a glass transparency is made from the negative and exposed onto a coated copper plate, leaving the image cut in relief. The dark areas of the design are then etched to retain the original photographic image. When printed, a photogravure looks like a photograph but is composed of a series of connected lines rather than the unconnected dots of a photograph.

Photomechanical

Those processes that cut an image into a surface by exposing photographic positives or negatives onto photosensitive material.

Pinxit or Pinx.

A Latin term meaning "has painted it."

Planographic

A printing process in which a design is drawn onto a stone or plate using a grease crayon or greasy ink. The printing ink is then absorbed into the greasy design on the stone and can be transferred to paper under light pressure.

Plate

A (metal) plate is a flat sheet, typically of copper, steel or zinc, which is used as a matrix. Metal plates are used for intaglio prints and some lithographs.

Plate Mark

The ridge left in the paper by the edge of an intaglio plate when printed.

Platinum Print

A process in which the paper is coated with a sensitized solution (mainly iron salts) and exposed to light. When exposed, the chemical processes leave a print of platinum (or palladium) that is embedded in the actual fibers of the paper, rather than in an emulsion coating the surface. The result is a delicate and very permanent image in tones of brown, gray, and black.

Plein Air
A late nineteenth century movement in France (literally "outside") that attempted to escape the confines of the studio and capture the spirit and colors of nature by painting outdoors.

Pochoir
A process in which a design is analyzed mechanically and broken into a series of stencils ("pochoirs"), which are used to apply layers of different color to an image after it has been printed.

Pop Art
A 1960s movement that reacted against abstraction by drawing on images from mass culture such as advertisements, comic strips, and consumer products.

Posterization
A special effect achieved in photography when light, medium and dark tones are documented in a series of time exposures, then made into separate screens and printed sequentially, resulting in "halos" of graded tones.

Post-Impressionism
Rejected the Impressionists' concern for naturalism and the effects of light in favor of increased expressionism, structure, and form.

Print
A single piece of paper upon which an image has been imprinted from a matrix.

Proof
An impression of a print pulled prior to the final published edition so that the artist can see what work still needs to be done to the matrix. A *trial* or *working proof* is one taken before the design on the matrix is finished. Once the printed image meets the artist's

expectations, this becomes a *bon à tirer* ("good to pull") *proof.* An *artist's proof* is an impression issued in addition to the regularly numbered edition and reserved for the artist's own use.

Provenance

The past history of a print, including when it was purchased and by whom, and also where it has been exhibited.

Publisher

The individual or firm that finances the printing and controls the marketing of an image.

Quarto

When a sheet of paper is folded into four equal parts, it produces a book known as a "quarto." The term can also refer to the individual paper size (each sheet measures approximately 9"x 12").

Rabbet

In framing, the groove in the molding that holds the glass and mat.

Rag Mat

A mat made of pure acid-free cotton rag. Can also be referred to as a *museum* or *conservation mat.*

Recto

The term designating the front of a piece of paper (or the right-hand page of an open book). *Verso* is the term for the back side of the paper (or the left-hand page of an open book).

References

Citations noted at the end of a catalogue raisonné entry that identify the author of the description and the number of the specific image. For example, the entry of a Piranesi engraving could be cited "Hind 82."

Registration

The marking and aligning of wood blocks so that the various colors will print exactly within the lines of the matrix block.

Relief
An image printed from a design raised above the surface of a block so that the image itself is slightly raised.

Remarque
A small vignette image in the margin of a print, often thematically related to the main image.

Reproduction
A copy of an original print, which can be made by hand or photomechanically.

Reserve
The minimum price that a seller will accept.

Restoration
The repair of damages (stains, spots, tears, holes) in a print.

Restrike
A later impression printed from an old block or plate that was not printed as part of the original publishing venture.

Rococo
This style developed in reaction to the heavy richness of the Baroque period with delicate details and a light, airy quality. Naturalistic elements such as shells and plants were often incorporated into rococo design.

Romanticism
A movement in the late eighteenth and early nineteenth centuries that rejected the order and balance of neo-classicism in favor of expressive, emotional, and imaginative images.

Roulette (Spur Wheel)
A tool used to produce texture on a metal plate.

School of
A phrase used to refer to the work of an unidentified artist who is closely associated with the named artist (although not necessarily his student).

Sculpsit or Sculp.
A Latin term meaning "has engraved it."

Secession
A group formed in Germany in the early twentieth century that moved to separate itself from the traditional art establishment.

Serigraph (Silk Screen)
A technique wherein ink or paint is pulled through a finely meshed fabric screen covered with a mask or stencil to create the image.

Sextodecimo
When a sheet of paper is folded into sixteen equal parts, it produces a book known as a "sextodecimo" or "sixteenmo." The term can also refer to the individual paper size (each sheet measures approximately 6" x 4").

Signed
A signed print is one signed, in pencil or ink, by the artist and/or engraver of the print at the time of publication. This signifies the artist's satisfaction with the workmanship and quality of the impression. Antique prints are signed only in the plate.

Sizing
The coating used to seal the surface of paper in order to provide a smooth, less absorbent surface to receive the ink.

Soft Ground Etching
A technique in which the metal plate is coated with a ground that never hardens and into which textured patterns can be impressed, producing a softer line.

State
A state of a print includes all the impressions pulled without any change being made to any aspect of the image. Also, it should be noted that states of a print are different from editions of a print. There can be several states of a print from the same edition, and there can be several editions of a print all with the same state.

Steel Engraving

A nineteenth-century development in intaglio printing that used steel for the matrix. The greater strength and durability of the plate made larger editions possible.

Stencil

Any kind of masking plate that has been cut with a hole or pattern of holes. The stencil is then placed directly on a sheet of paper and pigment is applied, producing an exact copy of the hole or design.

Stipple

A process of texturing wherein a spiked rocker ball or needle is used to cut multiple dots into an engraved plate.

Stone

A slab of stone, usually limestone, used as the surface for lithographic or chromolithographic images.

Suprematism

A purely abstract movement developed in Russia at the end of World War I which rejected objectivity by using square forms and eliminating color from the canvas.

Surrealism

A style originating in France in 1924 that attempted to create visual representations of the working of the subconscious mind. Some surrealists created realistic depictions of dreamlike states while others worked more in abstraction.

Technique

The process an artist chooses to achieve a desired effect.

Thermal Printing

A method of printmaking that creates an image in a pattern of small dots, using a waxy ink that produces stronger and clearer colors.

Trial Proof (T.P.)

An impression taken from a plate, block, stencil, or other print matrix to test how that particular image, or part of an image, will reproduce.

Tusche
The greasy ink used in drawing images on lithographic stones.

Verso
The term designating the back side of a piece of paper (or the left-hand page of an open book). See also *recto*.

Vetting
The examination of a piece by experts to verify that all information pertaining to the piece is correct.

Watermark
A design embossed into a piece of paper during its production and used to identify both the paper and the papermaker. The watermark can be seen when the paper is held up to light.

Woodblock
As in a woodcut, the design is drawn on wood and cut away with a knife or gouge to produce an outline (matrix) into which individual color blocks fit like puzzle pieces. The term "woodblock" is more commonly applied to eighteenth- and nineteenth-century Japanese prints.

Woodcut
A form of relief printing in which a piece of wood (usually the plank side of soft wood) is carved so that the raised areas carry ink to produce the design. A woodcut printed in color has a matrix block that outlines the entire image and then a separate block for each color.

Wood Engraving
A form of engraving in which the design is cut into a piece of end-grained hard wood rather than a metal plate.

WPA
Specifically referring to the Works Progress Administration, the massive employment program initiated by President Franklin D. Roosevelt's New Deal in 1935 (renamed the Work Projects Administration in 1939). Because a division of the program employed artists,

the term has come to be loosely associated with the art created under the WPA, works that celebrated American values and prosperity in an effort to combat pessimism that arose during the Depression.

Xerography
The modern method of photocopying commonly used in office copying machines. The process uses an electrostatic field to arrange grains of black ink into letters and images, which are then fixed by heat.

Zincography
A lithographic process that uses a zinc plate rather than a stone.

BIBLIOGRAPHY

The following is a list of reference books recommended for further exploration of subject matter, artists, and print processes.

REFERENCE

Bennett, Whitman. *A Practical Guide to American 19th Century Color Plate Books*. New York: Bennett Book Studios, 1949.

Fowble, E. McSherry. *Two Centuries of Prints in America, 1680–1880*. Charlottesville: University of Virginia Press, 1987.

Garrett, Albert. *A History of Wood Engraving*. London: Hacker Art Books, 1978.

Gascoigne, Bamber. *How to Identify Prints*. 2nd ed. New York: Thames & Hudson, 2004.

Griffiths, Antony. *Prints & Printmaking*. London: British Museum, 1980.

Hind, Arthur M. *A History of Engraving and Etching*. 3rd ed. New York: Dover, 1963.

Hind, Arthur M. *An Introduction to a History of Woodcut*. New York: Dover, 1953.

Horne, Alan J. *The Dictionary of 20th Century British Book Illustrators*. Woodbridge, Suffolk, England: Antique Collector's Club, 1994.

Houfe, Simon. *The Dictionary of 19th Century British Book Illustrators and Caricaturists*. Revised ed. Woodbridge, Suffolk, England: Antique Collector's Club, 1996.

Hults, Linda C. *The Print in the Western World: An Introductory History*. Madison: University of Wisconsin Press, 1996.

Ivins, William M. *How Prints Look*. Revised ed. Boston: Beacon Press, 1987.

Lepeltier, Robert. *The Restorer's Handbook of Drawings & Prints*. New York: Van Nostrand Reinhold, 1977.

MacKenzie, Ian. *British Prints: Dictionary and Price Guide*. New York: Apollo, 1988.

Mayor, Alpheus Hyatt. *Popular Prints of the Americas*. New York: Outlet, 1973.

Mayor, Alpheus Hyatt. *Prints and People: A Social History of Printed Pictures*. 3rd ed. Princeton: Princeton University Press, 1981.

McClinton, Katharine. *The Chromolithographs of Louis Prang*. New York: C. N. Potter (distributed by Crown Publishers), 1973.

Muir, Percy. *Victorian Illustrated Books*. New York: Chrysalis Books, 1989.

Nadeau, Luis. *Encyclopedia of Printing, Photographic, and Photomechanical Processes*. Fredericton, N.B., Canada: Atelier Luis Nadeau, 1989.

Peters, Herry T. *America on Stone: The Other Printmakers to the American People*. Manchester: Ayer Co. Publishers, 1976.

Porzio, Domenico. *Lithography: 200 Years of Art, History, and Technique*. Reprint edition. Secaucus, N.J.: Wellfleet Press, 1988.

Riggs, Timothy A. *The Print Council Index to Oeuvre—Catalogues of Prints by European and American Artists*. New York: Kraus International Publications, 1983.

Samuels, Harold and Peggy. *The Illustrated Biographical Encyclopedia of Artists of the American West*. New York: Doubleday, 1976.

Turner, Silvie. *Print Collecting*. New York: Lyons & Burford, 1996.

Wax, Carol. *The Mezzotint: History and Technique*. New York: Abrams, 1990.

Zigrosser, Carl. *A Guide to the Collecting and Care of Original Prints*. New York: Random House, 1965.

ARCHITECTURE

Copplestone, Trewin and Seton Lloyd. *World Architecture: An Illustrated History*. Revised ed. London: Hamlyn, 1966.

Dalzell, W. R. *Architecture: The Indispensable Art*.
London: Michael Joseph, 1962.

Hind, Arthur M. *Giovanni Battista Piranesi: A Critical
Study*. Reprint ed. New Castle: Oak Knoll Books,
1978.

Mayor, Alpheus Hyatt. *Giovanni Battista Piranesi*.
New York: H. Bittner and Co., 1952.

Millard, Mark J. *British Books: 17th–19th Century*.
Mark J. Millard Architectural Collection. Washington,
D.C.: Braziller, 1993.

————. *French Books: 16th–19th Century*. Mark J.
Millard Architectural Collection. Washington, D.C.:
Braziller, 1993.

————. *Italian and Spanish Books: 15th–19th
Century*. Mark J. Millard Architectural Collection.
Washington, D.C.: Braziller, 1993.

————. *Northern European Books: 16th–19th
Century*. Mark J. Millard Architectural Collection.
Washington, D.C.: Braziller, 1993.

Palladio, Andrea. *The Four Books of Architecture*.
New York: Dover, 1965.

Penny, Nicholas. *Piranesi*. London: Oresko Books
(distributed by Hippocrene Books), 1978.

Rabreau, Daniel. *Dessins d'Architecture Au Xviiie
Siecle*. Paris: Art Stock, 1996.

Weinreb, B. *Piranesi: Archaeologist and Vedutista*.
London: Weinreb Architectural Gallery, 1987.

Wilton-Ely, John. *Piranesi: The Complete Etchings*.
San Francisco: Alan Wofsy Fine Arts, 1994.

BIRDS

Audubon, John James. *Audubon's Birds of North
America*. Introduction by Sheila Buff. Stamford,
Conn.: Longmeadow Press, 1990.

De Battisti, Mariella. *John Gould's Birds*. Secaucus:
Chartwell Books, 1980.

John Gould's Hummingbirds. Secaucus, N.J.: Wellfleet, 1990.

Kastner, Joseph. *The Bird Illustrated, 1550–1900: From the Collections of the New York Public Library*. New York: Abrams, 1988.

Lambourne, Maureen. *Art of Bird Illustration*. New York: Knickerbocker Press, 1997.

McBurney, Henrietta. *Mark Catesby's Natural History of America*. Austin: University of Texas Press, 1997,

Peterson, Roger Tory, ed. *Audubon's Birds of America*. Revised ed. New York: Abbeville Press, 2003.

Sitwell, Sacheverell. *Fine Bird Books, 1700–1900*. Boston: Atlantic Monthly Press, 1990.

BOTANICALS

Aymonin, Gérard G. *Besler Florilegium*. New York: Abrams, 1989.

Besler, Basilius. *The Garden at Eichstatt*. New York: Taschen, 2000.

Blunt, Wilfrid. *The Art of Botanical Illustration: An Illustrated History*. New York: Dover, 1994.

Blunt, Wilfrid. *Tulipomania*. London: Penguin, 1950.

Clayton, Virginia Tuttle. *Gardens on Paper: Prints and Drawings, 1200–1900*. Philadelphia: University of Pennsylvania Press, 1999.

Dunthorne, Gordon. *Flower and Fruit Prints of the Eighteenth and Early Nineteenth Centuries*. New York: Da Capo Press, 1970.

Kaden, Vera C. *The Illustration of Plants & Gardens, 1500–1850*. London: Victoria and Albert Museum, 1982.

Kramer, Jack. *Women of Flowers*. New York: Stewart, Tabori & Chang, 1996.

Magnificent Botanical Books. London: Sotheby's, 1987.

Mallary, Frances, and Peter Mallary. *A Redouté Treasury: 468 Watercolors From Les Liliacées of Pierre-Joseph Redouté*. New York: Vendome Press, 1986.

McTigue, Bernard. *Nature Illustrated: Flowers, Plants, and Trees, 1550–1900*. New York: Abrams, 1989.

Raphael, Sandra. *An Oak Spring Sylva: A Selection of the Rare Books on Trees in the Oak Spring Garden Library*. Upperville, Va.: Oak Spring Garden Library (distributed by Yale University Press), 1989.

Raphael, Sandra. *An Oak Spring Pomona: A Selection of the Rare Books on Fruit in the Oak Spring Garden Library*. Upperville, Va.: Oak Spring Garden Library (distributed by Yale University Press), 1991.

Redouté, Pierre-Joseph. *The Lilies*. Cologne, Germany: Taschen, 2000.

Redouté, Pierre-Joseph. *Redouté's Roses*. Secaucus, N.J.: Wellfleet Press, 1990.

Rix, Martyn. *The Art of the Plant World: The Great Botanical Illustrators and Their Work*. New York: Viking Press, 1981.

Saunders, Gill. *Picturing Plants: An Analytical History of Botanical Illustration*. Berkeley: University of California Press, 1995.

Sitwell, Sacheverell, et al. *Great Flower Books, 1700–1900*. 2nd ed. Boston: Atlantic Monthly Press, 1990.

Tornasi, Lucia Tongiorgi. *An Oak Spring Flora: Flower Illustrations from the Fifteenth Century to the Present Time*. Upperville, Va.: Oak Spring Garden Library (distributed by Yale University Press), 1997.

CHILDREN'S

De Vries, Leonard. *Treasury of Illustrated Children's Books: Early Nineteenth Century Classics from the Osborne Collection*. New York: Abbeville Press, 1990.

Heppner, Darrell. *Great Children's Illustrators, 1880–1930*. Atglen, Pa.: Schiffer Publishing, 2004.

Holme, Bryan. *The Kate Greenaway Book*. New York: Penguin, 1977.

Meyer, Susan E. *Treasury of the Great Children's Book Illustrators*. New York: Abrams, 1997.

Postal, Edward S. *Price Guide and Bibliography to Children's & Illustrated Books*. Laguna Beach: M&P Press, 1995.

Targ, W. *Bibliophile in the Nursery*. Lanham, Md.: Scarecrow Press, 2000.

Wood, Christopher. *Fairies in Victorian Art*. Woodbridge, Suffolk, England: Antique Collector's Club, 2000.

CONSERVATION & RESTORATION

Dolloff, Francis and Roy Perkinson. *How to Care for Works of Art on Paper*. Boston: Museum of Fine Arts Boston, 1979.

Ellis, Margaret. *The Care of Prints and Drawings*. Nashville: AASLH Press (with assistance of Getty Trust), 1987.

COSTUME / FASHION

Ginsburg, Madeleine. *Paris Fashions: The Art Deco Style of the 1920s*. New York: Gallery Books, 1989.

Holland, Vyvyan. *Hand Coloured Fashion Plates, 1770–1899*. 2nd ed. London: B. T. Batsford Ltd., 1988.

Robinson, Julian. *The Golden Age of Style*. New York: Gallery Books, 1976.

Weill, Alain. *La Mode Parisienne*. Paris: Bibliothèque de l'Image, 2000.

JAPANESE

Forrer, Matthi. *The Baur Collection: Japanese Prints*. 2 vols. Geneva: Collections Baur, 1994.

Keyes, Roger S. *Japanese Woodblock Prints*. Bloomington: Indiana University Press, 1984.

Kobayashi, Tadashi. *Ukiyo-E: Great Japanese Art*. Tokyo: Kodansha International, 1982.

Lane, Richard. *Images from the Floating World*. New York: Dorset Press, 1982.

Michener, James A. *Japanese Prints*. Rutland, Vt.: Charles E. Tuttle Co., 1959.

Neuer, Roni and Herbert Libertson. *Ukiyo-E: 250 Years of Japanese Art*. New York: Mayflower Books, 1978.

Noguchi, Yone. *Hiroshige and Japanese Landscapes*. Tokyo: Japan Travel Bureau, 1954.

MANUSCRIPTS

De Hamel, Christopher. *Scribes and Illuminators*. Toronto: University of Toronto Press, 1992.

Whalley, Joyce. *The Art of Calligraphy*. London: Bloomsbury, 1980.

MAPS

Baynton-Williams, Roger. *Investing in Maps*. New York: C. N. Potter, 1969.

Brown, Lloyd A. *The Story of Maps*. New York: Dover, 1980.

Buisseret, David, ed. *From Sea Charts to Satellite Images: Interpreting North American History Through Maps*. Chicago: University of Chicago Press, 1990.

Burden, Philip D. *The Mapping of North America*. Rickmansworth, England: Raleigh Publications, 1996.

French, Josephine, ed. *Tooley's Dictionary of Mapmakers: A–D*. Revised ed. London: Map Collector Publications, 1999.

George, Wilma. *Animals & Maps*. London: Secker and Warburg, 1969.

Goss, John. *The Mapmaker's Art*. Chicago: Rand McNally, 1993.

Harley, J. Brian and David Woodward, eds. *The History of Cartography*. 2 vols. Chicago: University of Chicago Press, 1998.

King, Geoffrey. *Miniature Antique Maps: An Illustrated Guide for the Collector*. Tring, Hertfordshire, England: Map Collector Publications, 1996.

McLaughlin, Glen and Nancy H. Mayo. *The Mapping of California as an Island*. Saratoga: California Map Society, 1995.

Moreland, Carl and David Bannister. *Antique Maps*. 3rd ed. London: Phaidon Press, 1993.

Potter, Jonathan. *Collecting Antique Maps: An Introduction to the History of Cartography*. London: Jonathan Potter Ltd., 2002.

Shirley, R. W. *Mapping of the World, 1472–1700: Early Printed World Maps*. Albert Saifer Publisher, 1985.

Tooley, R. V. and Charles Bricker. *Landmarks of Mapmaking*. New York: Dorset Press, 1989.

Tooley, R. V. *Maps and Map-Makers*. 4th ed. New York: Bonanza, 1970.

Whitfield, Peter. *The Mapping of the Heavens*. London: The British Library Publishing, 1995.

MODERN

Art in Transition: Post-Impressionist Prints and Drawings from the Achenbach Foundation for the Graphic Arts. San Francisco: Fine Arts Museum of San Francisco, 1988.

Arwas, Victor. *Art Deco*. New York: Abrams, 1992.

Castleman, Riva. *Prints of the Twentieth Century: A History*. New York: Museum of Modern Art, 1976.

Eichenberg, Fritz. *Art of the Print: Masterpieces, History, Techniques*. New York: Abrams, 1976.

Ercoli, Giuliano. *Art Deco Prints*. New York: Rizzoli, 1989.

Hofstätter, Hans H. *Art Nouveau: Prints, Illustrations, and Posters*. New York: Greenwich House, 1984.

Ittmann, John W. *Post-Impressionist Prints: Paris in the 1890s*. Philadelphia: Philadelphia Museum of Art, 1998.

Leymarie, Jean and Michel Melot. *The Graphic Works of the Impressionists: Manet, Pissarro, Renoir, Cézanne, Sisley*. New York: Abrams, 1972.

Nineteenth and Twentieth Century Prints: The Selma Erving Collection. Northampton, Mass.: Smith College Museum of Arts, 1985.

Passeron, Roger. *Impressionist Prints*. New York: Dutton, 1974.

Robinson, Julian. *The Brilliance of Art Deco*. New York: Bartlet & Jensen, 1990.

Sachs, Paul J. *Modern Prints and Drawings: A Guide to Better Understanding of Modern Draughtsmanship*. New York: Knopf, 1954.

Schmutzler, Robert. *Art Nouveau*. New York: Abrams, 1962.

NATURAL HISTORY

Buchanan, Handasyde. *Nature into Art: A Treasury of Great Natural History Books*. New York: Mayflower, 1979.

Dance, S. Peter. *The Art of Natural History*. Woodstock: Overlook Press, 1978.

———. *Mammals (Classic Natural History Prints)*. New York: Chrysalis, 1991.

Kastner, Joseph. *The Animal Illustrated, 1550–1900*. New York: Abrams, 1991.

McBurney, Henrietta. *Mark Catesby's Natural History of America*. London: Merrell Publishers, 1997.

Olstein, Franklyn and Teresa Koziol, eds. *Audubon's Quadrupeds of North America*. Secaucus, N.J.: Wellfleet Press, 1989.

Wettengl, Kurt, ed. *Maria Sibylla Merian, 1647–1717: Artist and Naturalist*. Ostfildern, Germany: Hatje Cantz Publishers, 1998.

OCCUPATIONS

Gillespie, Charles C., ed. *A Diderot Pictorial Encyclopedia of Trades and Industry*. 2 vols. New York: Dover, 1959.

Karp, Diane R. *Ars Medica, Art, Medicine, and the Human Condition*. Philadelphia: University of Pennsylvania Press, 1985.

PORTRAITS

Cunningham, Noble E., Jr. *Popular Images of the Presidency: From Washington to Lincoln*. Columbia: University of Missouri Press, 1991.

Matthews, Roy T. and Peter Mellini. *In 'Vanity Fair'*. Berkeley: University of California Press, 1982.

Reaves, Wendy Wick, ed. *American Portrait Prints: Proceedings of the Tenth Annual American Print Conference*. Charlottesville: University of Virginia Press, 1984.

Russell, H. Diane and Bernadine Barnes. *Eva/Ave: Women in Renaissance and Baroque Prints*. New York: The Feminist Press at CUNY, 1999.

SOCIAL & POLITICAL

Abbey, J. R. *Life in England in Aquatint and Lithography, 1770–1860*. San Francisco: Alan Wofsy Fine Arts, 1991.

Buchanan-Brown, John. *The Book Illustrations of George Cruikshank*. Rutland, Vt.: Charles E. Tuttle Co., 1980.

Burke, Joseph and Colin Caldwell. *Hogarth: The Complete Engravings*. Secaucus, N.J.: Wellfleet Press, 1988.

Conningham, Frederic A. *Currier & Ives Prints: An Illustrated Check List*. New York: Crown Publishers, 1970.

Cuno, James. *French Caricature and the French Revolution, 1789–1799*. Los Angeles: Grunwald Center for the Graphic Arts, 1989.

Daumier Lithographs. New York: Reynal & Hitchcock, 1946.

Goldstein, Robert Justin. *Censorship of Political Caricature in Nineteenth-Century France*. Kent, Ohio: Kent State University Press, 1989.

Grandville, J. *Fantastic Illustrations of Grandville*. New York: Dover, 1988.

Hayes, John. *The Art of Thomas Rowlandson*. Alexandria, Va.: Art Services International, 1990.

Houfe, Simon. *The Dictionary of British Book Illustrators and Caricaturists, 1800–1914*. Woodbridge, Suffolk, U.K.: Antique Collectors' Club, 1978.

Paston, George. *Social Caricature in the 18th Century*. New York: Benjamin Blom, 1968.

Paulson, Ronald. *Hogarth (Vol. I): The 'Modern Moral Subject,' 1697–1732*. New Brunswick, N.J.: Rutgers University Press, 1991.

Paulson, Ronald. *Hogarth (Vol. II): High Art and Low, 1732–1750*. New Brunswick, N.J.: Rutgers University Press, 1992.

Paulson, Ronald. *Hogarth: His Life, Art, and Times*. Abridged ed. New Haven: Yale University Press, 1974.

Peters, Harry T. *Currier & Ives: Printmakers to the American People*. New York: Doubleday, Doran, & Co., 1942.

Rawls, W. *The Great Book of Currier & Ives' America*. New York: Abbeville Press, 1979.

Samuels, Harold and Peggy Samuels. *Remington: The Complete Prints*. New York: Crown Publishing, 1990.

St. Hill, Thomas Nast. *Thomas Nast: Cartoons and Illustrations*. New York: Dover, 1974.

West, Richard Samuel. *Satire on Stone: The Political Cartoons of Joseph Keppler*. Chicago: University of Illinois Press, 1988.

SPORTING

Arlott, John and Arthur Daley. *Pageantry of Sport*. New York: Hawthorn, 1968.

Lane, Charles. *Sporting Aquatints and Their Engravers*. Leigh-on-Sea, England: F. Lewis Publishers, 1978.

Podeschi, John B. *Books on the Horse and Horsemanship, Riding, Hunting, Breeding, and Racing,*

1400–1941. New Haven: Yale Center for British Art, 1981.

Walker, Stella A. *Sporting Art England, 1700–1900*. New York: C. N. Potter, 1972.

SPECIAL SUBJECT: NATIVE AMERICANS

Bodmer, Karl. *Karl Bodmer's America*. Lincoln: University of Nebraska Press, 1984.

Gilreath, James, et al. *The North American Indian Portfolios: From the Library of Congress*. Reprint ed. New York: Abbeville Press, 1993.

Horan, James David. *North American Indian Portraits: 120 Full-Color Plates from the McKenney-Hall Portrait Gallery*. New York: Crown, 1975.

McCracken, Harold. *George Catlin and the Old Frontier*. New York: Dial Press, 1959.

Moore, Robert J. *Native Americans: The Art and Travels of Charles Bird King, George Catlin, and Karl Bodmer*. New York: Stewart, Tabori & Chang, 1997.

Thomas, David H., and Lorann Pendleton, eds. *Native Americans*. Alexandria, Va.: Time-Life, 1999.

Viola, Herman J. *After Columbus: The Smithsonian Chronicle of the North American Indians*. Washington, D.C.: The Smithsonian Institution Press, 1993.

TOPOGRAPHY

Abbey, J. R. *Scenery of Great Britain and Ireland*. San Francisco: Alan Wofsy Fine Arts, 1991.

Berkvam, Michael L., and Sean Shesgreen. *Eighteenth Century Cities: A Panorama*. Bloomington, Ind.: The Lilly Library, Indiana University, 1983.

Dawdy, Doris Ostrander. *Artists of the American West*. Chicago: Sage Books, 1974.

Leek, Michael E. *The Art of Nautical Illustration*. Secaucus, N.J.: Wellfleet Press, 1992.

Meinig, D. W. *The Shaping of America: A Geographical Perspective on 500 Years of History*. Reprint ed. New Haven: Yale University Press, 1988.

Reps, John W. *Views and Viewmakers of Urban America*. Columbia: University of Missouri Press, 1984.

Rossi, Paul A. *Art of the Old West*. New York: Knopf, 1971.

Taft, Robert. *Artists and Illustrators of the Old West*. New York: Charles Scribner's Sons, 1953.

Tyler, Ron. *Prints of the West*. Golden, Colo.: Fulcrum Publishing, 1994.

TRAVEL & VOYAGES

Abbey, J. R. *Travel in Aquatint and Lithography, 1770–1860*. 2 vols. San Francisco: Alan Wofsy Fine Arts, 1991.

Adams, Percy G. *Travelers and Travel Liars, 1660–1800*. New York: Dover, 1980.

Crone, Gerald Roe. *The Voyages of Discovery*. New York: Putnam, 1970.

Goetzmann, William H. *New Lands, New Men: America and the Second Great Age of Discovery*. New York: Viking Press, 1986.

Joppien, Rudiger and Bernard Smith. *The Art of Cook's Voyages*. Oxford: Oxford University Press, 1987.

Lorant, Stefan, ed. *The New World: The First Pictures of America*. New York: Duell, Sloan, and Pearce, 1946.

Poesch, Jessie. *Titian Ramsay Peale and His Journals of the Wilkes Expedition, 1799–1885*. Philadelphia: The American Philosophical Society, 1961.

Roberts, David and Fabio Bourbon. *Egypt: Yesterday and Today*. Cairo: American University in Cairo Press, 2001.

Roberts, David and Fabio Bourbon. *The Holy Land: Yesterday and Today*. Cairo: American University in Cairo Press, 2001.

Viola, Herman. *Magnificent Voyagers: The U.S. Exploring Expedition, 1838–1842*. Washington, D.C.: Smithsonian Books, 1985.

Ward, Geoffrey C. *The West: An Illustrated History*. New York: Book Sales, 1996.

MARKET TRENDS

Throughout the previous chapters, we have been discussing the various factors that affect both the availability of prints and their prices in the art market. Perhaps it would be helpful to look at current trends in today's art market. In the last decade, despite economic fluctuations, there has been a slow but steady appreciation of both antique and modern prints. As is to be expected, some artists (particularly contemporary printmakers) are somewhat overpriced while others like Picasso are still a good value. Likewise, in the antique print market, Audubon's elephant folio birds and Redouté's roses have topped out while Martinet's exotic birds and Weinmann botanical images are still relatively reasonable. You might find it helpful now to look at the price range of a few specific prints. Remember to keep in mind that the value of any specific print depends on the quality and condition of that particular image.

Untitled Castle Scene by Verard. Metalcut
15th century   *$985–$1285*

Untitled Battle Scene for Brabant Chronicle
15th century   *$485–$685*

Pisa for rare German edition of the *Nuremberg Chronicle* by Wolgemuth. Woodcut
15th century   *$685–$885*

Tilling the Fields for Virgil's *Georgics* by Unknown Artist. Woodcut
16th century   *$685–$985*

Proserpine by Goltzius. Chiaroscuro woodcut
16th century   *$2250–$2850*

Christ Before Caiaphas for *Small Passion* by Dürer. Engraving
16th century   *$2880–$3880*

Bust of Man Wearing a High Cap by Rembrandt. Etching
17th century   *$4500–$6000*

Batavian Expedition to China by Meursium. Engraving
17th century   *$485–$685*

Mülier Wiennensis by Hollar. Etching
17th century   *$327–$485*

Daffodils for *Florilegium* by Sweert. Engraving
17th century $1250–$1587

**Map of Scotia for *Theatre of Great Britain* by Speed.
Engraving**
17th century $3885–$4885

**Butterflies & Lemons for *Insectorium Surinamensium*.
Engraving**
17th century $3485–$3885

La Naissance d'Amour by Haid. Mezzotint
18th century $685–$885

French Family Dancing by Rowlandson. Aquatint
18th century $985–$1285

Lady Mary Campbell by Ramsay. Stipple engraving
18th century $485–$685

**Teatro Olympico for *Quattro Libri d' Architectura* by
Scamozzi. Engraving**
18th century $485–$685

Narcissus for Hortus Eystettensis by Besler. Engraving
17th century $3885–$4885

The Election by Hogarth. Engraving
18th century $685–$885

Les Infants de Bacchus by Watteau. Etching
18th century $1480–$1800

Diverse Orbis Terre by Schenk. Engraving
18th century $6800–$8000

Manakin Birds by Martinet. Engraving
18th century $385–$485

**Tulips for *Phantanthoza Iconographia* by Weinmann.
Mezzotint**
18th century $2800–$3800

**Night Dance in Hapaee (Cook's Islands) for *Capt.
Cooke's Third Voyage* by Weber. Engraving**
18th century $485–$685

**Paris Bird & Ligistrium for *Natural History of Georgia
& the Carolina's* by Catesby. Engraving**
18th century $2485–$2850

Busts of Two Geishas by Utamaro. Woodblock
18th century $2285–$2850

**Arco di Septimo Servo for *Vedute de Roma* by Piranesi.
Etching**
18th century $3885–$4885

**Greek Vase Fragments for *Hamilton's Antiquities* by
Flaxman. Engraving**
19th century $685–$985

Fleur d'Orangier for *Fleurs Animées* by Grandville. Lithograph
19th century $125–$185

Le Dimanche au Jardin des Plantes for *Charivari* by Daumier. Lithograph
19th century $125–$185

***Yosemite* by Prang. Chromolithograph**
19th century $185–$285

***Morte d' Arthur* by Beardsley. Linocut**
19th century $685–$985

Imperial Palace for *Manners & Customs of China* by Allom. Engraving
19th century $165–$225

Slenidera Gouldi Toucan for *Monograph on Toucans* by Gould. Lithograph
19th century $2885–$3485

Northern Hare for *Quadrupeds of North America* (Elephant Folio) by Audubon. Lithograph
19th century $3885–$4885

***English Wild Flowers* by Loudon. Lithograph**
19th century $385–$485

Chippewa Squaw for *North American Indians* by McKenny & Hall. Lithograph
19th century $985–$1285

***One Hundred Views of Provinces* by Hiroshige. Woodblock**
19th century $1885–$2485

***Geisha with Umbrella* by Toyokuni III. Woodblock**
19th century $485–$685

***Un Seigneur du Temps de François* 1 by Delacroix. Etching and drypoint**
19th century $1285–$1585

***Les Gitanos* by Manet. Etching**
19th century $3485–$3885

***The Pursuit* by Currier & Ives. (Large folio) lithograph**
19th century $1850–$2285

Tichborne Trial for *Harper's Weekly*. Wood Engraving
19th century $485–$685

"Saved by the skin of..." for *Harper's* Weekly by Nast. Wood Engraving
19th century $85–$125

***Souvenir d' Italie* by Corot. Etching**
19th century $1885–$2285

Portrait du Peintre A. Guillaumin Pendu by Cézanne. Etching
19th century $1585–$2585

Doorway and Vines by Whistler. Etching
19th century $1885–$2285

The Kiss by Behrens. Woodcut
19th century $2485–$3000

Panurge by Leander. Lithograph
20th century $485–$685

Yvette Guilbert by Toulouse-Lautrec. Lithograph
19th century $2500–$3500

Femme Nue Couche by Renoir. Etching
20th century $1585–$1885

Der Polster by Kurzweil. Color woodcut
20th century $585–$885

Grand Canyon of Arizona after Moran. Chromolithograph
20th century $3885–$4885

Le Faune by Picasso. Aquatint
20th century $6000–$8500

Odalisque by Matisse. Color lithograph
20th century $6000–$8500

Réincarnations du Père Ubu by Rouault. Etching and aquatint
20th century $1500–$2000

Connoisseurs of Prints by Sloan. Etching
20th century $6000–$8500

Oiseau Multicolore by Braque. Color lithograph
20th century $6000–$8500

Tetlow I by Feininger. Etching
20th century $600–$900

Nachdenkende de Frau by Kollwitz. Lithograph
20th century $1350–$2250

Akt mit Facher by Chagall. Etching and drypoint
20th century $3000–$3700

La Peche by Dufy. Woodcut
20th century $300–$500

Girls at Counter by Bishop. Etching
20th century $475–$675

Sueño by Rivera. Lithograph
20th century $10,000–$12,000

The Fence Mender by Benton. Lithograph
20th century $2000–$3000

Descending by Bibelk. Serigraph
20th century   *$3000–$3500*

Group Portrait with Dog & Cat by Sekino. Woodblock
20th century   *$2500–$3000*

Winter in Aizu by Saito. Woodblock
20th century   *$1200–$1800*

Untitled Landscape by Munakata. Woodblock
20th century   *$2800–$4000*

Supermarket by Shahn. Silkscreen
20th century   *$3500–$4500*

Etchings & Drypoints by Diebenkorn. Aquatint and
drypoint
20th century   *$4000–$6000*

Campbell's Soup Can on Shopping Bag by Warhol.
Silkscreen
20th century   *$4000–$5000*

Sunrise by Lichtenstein. Offset lithograph
20th century   *$5000–$8000*

Circus by Miró. Lithograph
20th century   *$4000–$5000*

Gardens of Rome by Vignal. Collotype
20th century   *$685–$985*

Stage Set by Craig. Gravure
20th century   *$65–$125*

Peter Pan in Kensington Gardens by Rackham. Offset
20th century   *$85–$125*

Anemone by Foord. Pochoir
20th century   *$325–$485*

Germany, The Land of Music by Von Axter. Lithograph
20th century   *$385–$485*

Stage Set for Macbeth by Stern. Serigraph
20th century   *$125–$185*

Shaman by Fay. Monotype
20th century   *$2800–$4800*

Picabia II by Dine. Mixed media
20th century   *$6000–$10,000*

INDEX

Page numbers in italics refer to illustrations and captions.

ABOUT THE AUTHOR

Leila Phee Lyons is a partner in the firm of Lyons Ltd. Antique Prints located in the historic Town & Country Village at the foot of Stanford University in Palo Alto, California. She has written and lectured extensively on period graphics, is frequently cited in national publications, and appears on House and Garden Television. Exhibiting nationally since 1968, Lyons Ltd. has specialized in original etchings, engravings, and lithographs dating from 1490 to 1920. In addition, Dr. & Mrs. Lyons have an extensive personal collection of antique and modern graphics acquired in their world travels. Lyons is past president of the California Antique Dealers Association and a member of the Art & Antique Dealers League of America, the Confédération Internationale des Négociants en Oeuvres d'Art, the Antiques Council, and the International Society of Appraisers.